LOLA BERRY'S
SUMMER FOOD

To my mum, thank you
for always supporting me
even when I don't realise it.
It really means the world
and I love you to
the moon and back.

LOLA BERRY'S
SUMMER FOOD

60+ fresh recipes and simple detox tips
to kickstart your summer

plum.   Pan Macmillan Australia

Contents

Introduction

The Beatles' 'Here Comes the Sun' is probably my favourite song, and its lyrics are the only tattoo I've ever wanted to get. There's just something magical about them. Like the song, summer to me is full of awesome energy and love. We can let the heaviness of winter go and get outside and really soak up what's out there. It's a time for going on adventures, trying something new, getting amongst nature and really getting in tune with our bodies. It's a great time to achieve our health goals, too, as it's much easier to get out and be active when it's warm and sunny.

Often summer is seen as a time to indulge over Christmas and New Year. Now, of course it's wonderful to celebrate and feast with our loved ones, but it's about doing that with foods that the body thrives off. Summer is a time to nourish yourself, to eat seasonally and to enjoy every bite. What's more festive than that?

I love the food of summer – it's bright, light and always delicious, and makes the traditional 'summer detox' a much easier prospect. When I refer to a detox, I'm not talking about some gruelling regime, but rather a series of simple steps like upping your fluids, eating more greens, making smart food swaps and cutting down on or quitting alcohol and caffeine for a time. Most importantly, detoxing means eating light and nourishing wholefood-based meals that really make you feel clear, crisp and fresh.

This little summer book will help you do just that: it's full of festive salads, drinks, brekkies and light treats that will give your body the energy it needs to thrive. There are also a few easy steps you can take to detox your body and mind without necessarily changing your whole lifestyle. When I go on a summer detox, I still want to go out and have a social life without feeling like I'm missing out on everything. So we're talking simple steps to help you feel your best that are a walk in the park to implement. I know you've got this, so now's the time to put yourself first and become the best version of you.

Mini summer detox

When we do a cleanse or detox we expect it to be hardcore and really restrictive, but I truly believe if you want long-term results then it's more about small changes that don't make you feel like you're missing out on your favourite things. This makes it so much easier to stick to until you get the results you're after.

The following are just a few simple tips and tricks to kickstart a mini summer cleanse. You can implement these without drastically changing your diet, and any recipe from this book will fit into this cleanse. Rather than thinking about detoxing, think about enjoying this new way of living!

Simple detox tips:

- Start your day with lemon juice in warm water. Simply squeeze half a fresh lemon into a small glass of water, filling the glass to about a third, then have it like a shot. Try not to sip on it or swish it about in your mouth, as the acid can erode the enamel of your teeth. The warm water coupled with the lemon juice will help to stimulate your liver, which is one of the body's major detox organs.
- Drink 2–3 litres of water per day. The first sign of dehydration is hunger, so keeping hydrated will also help keep a lid on cravings.
- Up your greens. Think broccoli, kale, silverbeet, spinach, asparagus, brussels sprouts – even though they're more wintery – mustard greens … even salad mixes will do the trick. Green juices are the easiest way to do this (they're high in fibre and nutritionally dense). Plus, when you're going through a detox it can be easier to stress out at the start, and green things are full of magnesium which helps to calm the nervous system.
- Have one vegetarian meal a day. In fact, having one completely veggo day a week is a great way to not only give your digestive system a break but also to cut down your meat consumption without going too extreme. (If you're a strict paleo and think missing out on complete protein for one day is no good, remember that back in caveman times there would be the odd day where they wouldn't have a successful hunt and would have had to skip meat!)
- Drink cleansing teas such as nettle and dandelion to support both liver and kidney detoxification. Milk thistle (St Mary's thistle) also supports liver detoxing and is brilliant to take after a big night out for this reason. You can drink it as a tea or take it in supplement form.
- Count colours … and I'm not talking Skittles! Think about counting different fruits and veggies, which give you a broad spectrum of phytochemicals (plant nutrients). For example, red things contain lycopene and green things contain chlorophyll and magnesium, and both are brilliant for our health.

- Make smart food swaps (gluten-free alternatives for wheat, nut milk for cow's milk, coconut sugar for white sugar, raw chocolate for the dairy-based stuff). Doing this will mean that your diet contains fewer foods that can cause inflammation, making it easier to cleanse and, if weight loss is desired, lose unwanted weight too.

- Listen to your body. According to Chinese medicine, different parts of your body detox at different times of night while you sleep, e.g. 11 pm–1 am is gall bladder and 1–3 am is your liver. So if you find you wake up between 1 and 3 am, it can be a sign that your liver needs a little support.

- Cut down on or quit alcohol for a month. Not only will this give your liver a break, it will also help to get your mind clear, and help you have more willpower when it comes to staying on track. Alcohol weakens discipline – think about that 'hangover meal' you have the next day! So cutting back on the drinks means you stay focused. That said, if you do still want to enjoy a drink, pick healthier options that won't undo all your hard work. Think clear spirits like vodka or gin and ask for them to be mixed with

soda water and fresh lemon or lime juice (not the packet stuff, with added sugars and preservatives). If you're making drinks at home, fresh or frozen berries can give your drinks a refreshing zing and sweetness. Try vodka, fresh lemon juice, strawberries and sparkling mineral water – clean and delicious – or your choice of clear spirit with one of the spritzers on page 149. I'm not a massive drinker, but to help prevent a hangover and keep myself on track the next day, I like to take vitamin B and liver detox supplements before and after drinking alcohol, as well as making sure I drink plenty of water during and after drinking to prevent dehydration.

- Cut down on caffeine. Try to halve the amount you have; so if it's four coffees a day try to gradually get down to two. And if it's one a day then try replacing it with a green tea. Coffee in moderation is full of antioxidants, which remain intact when exposed to heat, so I'm all for coffee in the diet. But when it becomes something you rely on just to get through the day it's time to pull back and potentially decrease your caffeine intake.

- Surround yourself with detoxing crystals and colours for cleansing and new beginnings. See my handy guide on page 12.
- Get rid of all treats and temptations, or gift them to someone if you don't want to waste them. Trust me, you will eat whatever is in the house, so you want to set up an environment that will help you succeed.
- Stay motivated by making it easier on yourself. Put your exercise gear out the night before so you don't have to think about whether or not to train – it's much easier if it's just a given that you will train when you wake up. Or pack your gym gear in the car so you can exercise after work if you're an afternoon trainer.
- Make sure you individualise any cleanse or detox to suit you. This one is really important! Try to find ways to treat yourself other than unhealthy food; like going to the movies, or for juice and smoothie dates. Things that don't make you feel like you're missing out. I love drinking a calming tea at night and watching an episode of my favourite show, and I also love going on nature walks – they're just little things I do for me. It's about tailoring a detox so it works for you; that way you'll be more inclined to stick to it.
- Remove your roadblocks. One of mine is staying up too late then finding I'm really hungry the next day, so sleep is key. I stop looking at my laptop at least an hour before I want to go to sleep, so the blue light isn't affecting my body's production of melatonin – the hormone that helps control your sleeping and waking cycles – which can make falling asleep quite tricky. Your phone has this same blue light, but there are now apps and setting updates which can alter this to reduce the impact on melatonin production. That said, I still try to stay off my phone before bed, even if I do occasionally find myself sneaking onto instagram or snapchat for one last peek before going to sleep!
- Be happy! If you're not happy it becomes so hard to stick to eating clean. The reality is we're not always happy, but you can choose to do everything in your power to do things that make you happy: music, movies, nature, seeing mates, yoga, laughter, a roadtrip, walking the dog …

Crystals and colours

✳

Crystals do more than just look pretty; they have been used in healing for aeons. It is believed that crystals can hold and affect energy. I am definitely drawn to crystals, and having them around me and learning about them is something that I love.

When you buy a new crystal it will have the energy of the people it's been around, so I always like to cleanse it as soon as I bring it home. There are a few different methods you can try, such as washing it in salt water (this can cause the breakdown of some crystals, though, so ask for the best way to cleanse your crystals when purchasing). My favourite method is to burn frankincense around my crystals and ask that they be cleansed with love.

Colours can also have a huge impact on our mental and emotional states. You can take this with a grain of salt, but if it resonates with you then why not try it? It can be the colours you choose to wear or the colours you surround yourself with. Fresh, bright flowers are a great way to instantly bring colour therapy into your world without needing to redecorate.

Best crystals for detoxing:
- **Amethyst** is said to strengthen the immune system, stimulate metabolism – which is great if you want to increase the rate at which your body burns off energy – cleanse the blood and help with addictions. Amethyst may also help with headaches, which are often a side effect of doing any kind of detox, especially if you're pulling back on coffee – just hold a piece of amethyst where you feel the pain. Finally, amethyst is said to be an important crystal for the nervous system, so it is great for calming you down when you're stressed out.
- **Malachite** is traditionally used to help reduce pain and inflammation. When we detox there's often what's called a 'detox response', in which symptoms can become worse before they get better – and this can arise in the form of inflammation. Malachite is also great for relieving fluid retention, helping with sleep and strengthening the immune system.
- **Bloodstone** is another goodie for healing and detoxing. It is said to boost the immune system, cleanse the blood, stimulate the metabolism and is great for kidney health, too.
- **Turquoise** is a big healer and can enhance detoxification. It helps to change addictive patterns with food, alcohol, smoking and drugs. It is also a great one for combating pain: I have a sensitive stomach and will often hold this crystal on my tummy to help ease the pain and inflammation.

Best colours for detoxing:
- **White** promotes the healing of the body, mind and spirit. It's a cleanser on all levels and is said to be a natural pain reliever. It also helps to get rid of negative energy.
- **Yellow** is bright and uplifting; it's the colour of happiness. It's great for reducing stress, and when we're detoxing it's really easy to stress out in the beginning.
- **Green** is your super healing colour. This one is all about cleansing and new beginnings, allowing the body to heal in its own way.
- **Brown** is said to help you deal with sorrow and absorb pain, bringing us grounding and strength.

Positive affirmations for detoxing

The way we talk to ourselves in our minds has a huge impact on whether or not we can stick to a detox. I can promise you, while I'm self-loathing I can never stay on track – it's the perfect way to self-sabotage your goals. So think about positive affirmations and, if it helps, write them down. I do! I have a 'manifesto book' in which I write all of my goals and dreams, and I write them in the present tense as if they've already happened. That really sets the tone of success: it's like it's already done in your mind, and you're then simply trusting it will come to fruition.

I am
happy

I am the
best version
of myself

I am
healthy

I feel
amazing

I love
who
I am

I feel
cleansed

Summer kickstart:
a sample day

People always ask me what I eat and how much I exercise on any given day.
The following is a pretty typical summer day in the life of me.

7 am: Wake up, lemon juice in warm water (page 8)

7.30 am: Exercise (walk/jog/yoga)

8.30 am: Brekkie: Lamington Granola (page 44) with almond milk and raspberry–chia jam,
plus an optional scoop of whey or vegan protein powder for extra protein

10 am: Morning snack: Crispy Kale Chippies (page 70), plus chopped raw vegetables
(carrot, capsicum, cucumber, celery) and hummus if you're really hungry

12.30 pm: Lunch: Raw Vegan Zucchini Pasta with Basil Pesto (page 86 – can be leftovers from
the night before) with some extra protein, such as poached chicken breast, if you like

3 pm: Afternoon snack: Happy Hearts Trail Mix (page 64) to help with that afternoon sugar
craving and give you a chocolate hit

6 pm: Dinner: Superfood Crispy Salmon Stir-fry (page 112) with leftovers saved to make
a brilliant lunch for the next day

8 pm: Evening treat: Blissed Out Berry and Apple Crumble (page 133), saving some for brekkie
the next day, or a cup of tea and an Aussie Super Ball (page 63), or simply a handful of nuts,
depending on how your body is feeling (listen to it, it will tell you what it's after).

The power of the sun

Biophilia would have to be my favourite word in the entire world. We're talking about the healing power of Mother Nature, and to me it makes total sense. We are innately drawn to being outside and in nature, especially as kids. There's something really freeing about it: when you're in nature and around other living organisms you see things more clearly, you gain perspective and little things don't seem to bother you as much. The judgemental and materialistic stuff just falls to the side. It doesn't matter any more. Life seems real and it is much easier to live from the heart. This is no coincidence.

Sunshine has been used since ancient times as a healing device. It is said that some monks even fasted on sunshine, and that's how they made their energy, so there must be something pretty special about it! Now to be clear, I'm not saying to go out and get scorched – that's way too much – but healthy exposure to the sun, particularly the vitamin D it contains, is an essential element when it comes to being happy and healthy. Not only does it increase the amount of serotonin – the neurochemical associated with happiness – your brain produces, it is also important for healthy skin and balanced hormones. Furthermore, you need sunlight to help regulate your circadian rhythm (your biological clock) and ensure you sleep well at night.

When I lived on the Gold Coast, most mornings I'd get up and walk our dog Croissant – he was a French bulldog so we thought the name was pretty fitting – on the beach in Burleigh Heads at sunrise. I would look up at the sun and say 'thank you', realising just how lucky I was to be healthy enough to be walking this cute little pooch on this picture-perfect beach. I would set my intention for the day, and I loved that moment of acknowledging Mother Nature and the sun. It was pretty special: almost like a meditation of sorts, which could set the tone for the entire day. The power of the sun is truly awesome.

Combine the sun and the sea and you have something very special indeed. A quick dip in the ocean can change how I'm feeling; to me, the ocean is so restful. Scientists think that this has something to do with the expanse of sky and water, which gives our brains a rest. And because we can float easily in salt water, we feel light and free. I try to get to the beach as much as possible in the summer months because I feel so centred, clear and rejuvenated there, and the silver lining is that it gives me mermaid hair!

But in all seriousness, even if you're not a swimmer, just walking in the water makes a huge difference and helps to put things into perspective. I always set intentions in the water; it makes me trust and know that there's a much bigger plan in store for us all and everything happens for a reason. The bottom line is to get out and soak up Mother Nature, and while you're there, thank her. Remember that you are so lucky to have the freedom to be where you are in your life. You have freedom of choice and the fact you're choosing to eat well and look after yourself is a luxury. When you come from this place it's not so hard to want to honour yourself.

Staying hydrated

The truth is that most of us are dehydrated and need to be drinking more water, and this is even more important in summer when the weather is hot. I'm guilty of not drinking enough too: I've just skulled a massive glass of water after realising I haven't drunk enough today! Aim for 1 litre of water per day for every 22 kilograms of body weight. So if you weigh 66 kilos that's 3 litres of water. It may sound like a lot, but the key is to start gradually and work your way up — otherwise you'll be running to the loo every ten minutes! (Note that herbal teas count towards your water intake, but not soups, smoothies, juices, coffee or caffeinated teas.)

Water is critically important for the healthy functioning of the human body. If we don't have enough of it, our skin becomes dry, it can be much harder to focus and we might not be as regular on the loo, to name just a few signs of poor hydration. Did you know that the first sign of dehydration is hunger? Interestingly, headaches at the front of the head can be caused by dehydration, so next time you have a frontal headache, try the glass-of-water trick!

Keeping those fluids up is easy if you have a glass or bottle of water at your desk. I use a glass, swing-top bottle — or a clear BPA-free plastic one — so I can see how much I'm drinking, but a good-quality stainless steel or aluminium container is just as good. Getting the fluid into your body is the important thing.

People often tell me that they can't bear the thought of having to drink so much water because they find the taste so boring. If this is you, get creative with your water by adding mint leaves, berries — both frozen and fresh work — or thin slices of lemon, orange and/or lime (don't squeeze in any citrus juice as it can erode tooth enamel if you're sipping on it all day). Even cucumber slices taste great in a bottle of water!

Natural summer beauty

❋

These natural beauty tips are all super-easy and cheap, and they really do work!

Hair

- Use Australian extra-virgin olive oil or extra-virgin coconut oil on the mid-length and ends of your hair as a moisturiser and to prevent split ends, but not on the roots because it's really hard to remove. Leave in for at least 10 minutes, or overnight if your hair is very dry. After any oil treatment, massage shampoo through your hair while it's still dry then jump in the shower and add water – this helps the shampoo cut through the oil.

- Eat foods that are high in natural fats and zinc. Extra-virgin olive oil, coconut oil, avocados, eggs, deep-sea fish and raw nuts and seeds are all high in natural fats and promote glossy hair. Zinc helps stimulate growth and prevent dandruff. Zinc is found in nuts, seeds, red meat, eggs and dried figs.

- Supplement with silica, a mineral that is known to strengthen connective tissues, meaning it's great for your hair and makes it shinier. You'll find loads of silica products at your local health-food store.

Face

- Drink plenty of water! Hydration is key.

- A little sunshine will give you that healthy glow (and boost your vitamin D levels). Don't go overboard here as sun exposure also causes free radical damage, and therefore ages the skin. There are loads of great organic sunscreens out there; try them out until you find the right fit for you.

- Coconut oil on the face and neck is a wonderful, rich moisturiser.

- Homemade masks are amazing. I make them with mashed avocado, honey and raw cacao, and will add cacao nibs or steel-cut oats if I want a gentle exfoliation. I always pack a mask when I travel; it's a great way to build in a little health retreat wherever I go.

- Foods high in natural fats are your skin's best friend: raw nuts, seeds, avocado, deep-sea fish, even eggs. Then you want to up the antioxidants, so go nuts on the berries and brightly coloured fruits and veggies. Antioxidants help to prevent free radical damage and skin ageing.

- I use raw tomato, cucumber or potato discs topically on sunburn, then coconut oil following a cold shower (a cold shower will literally help your skin stop cooking). Cold chamomile tea bags are also great used topically on sunburn.

Body

- Body scrubs can help to get rid of cellulite. I use a coffee body scrub; the smell alone is uplifting (see my recipe on page 24)!

- Post-sun, use coconut oil, extra-virgin olive oil and aloe vera.

- On the body generally, I use a combo of extra-virgin olive oil and coconut oil.

- For body odour issues, try drinking fennel tea to promote 'odourless perspiration'.

- For smelly feet, try soaking them in a bucket of warm water with four bags of black tea. The tannins in the tea help get rid of the nasty smell due to the astringent effect they have on the body.

Homemade summer beauty treatments

Store all of the following oil-based treatments in glass jars rather than plastic containers, so that the fats won't absorb anything nasty from the plastic. Dark glass is especially good as it will help prevent the ingredients from oxidising, meaning these little beauties will last even longer.

Coffee scrub

Minimises cellulite and stimulates circulation. The lavender oil is also brilliant for stretch marks. This will last for months.

25 g (⅓ cup) ground coffee
60 g (⅓ cup) brown sugar
125 ml (½ cup) extra-virgin olive oil
2–3 drops of peppermint essential oil
2–3 drops of lavender essential oil

Mix the ingredients together thoroughly and store in a sealed glass jar until needed. To use, rub the scrub in a circular motion all over your body, or just into the problem areas. This works best on a wet body, so I jump in the shower and turn the water off while I exfoliate, then turn the water back on to rinse off.

Body butter

Moisturises and helps prevent skin ageing. The raw cacao is full of antioxidants. Stored in a jar out of direct sunlight, this will keep for ages (I've had some of my creations for over a year).

115 g (½ cup) shea butter
115 g (½ cup) cocoa butter
125 ml (½ cup) coconut oil, melted
125 ml (½ cup) extra-virgin olive oil
30 g (¼ cup) raw cacao powder
2–3 drops of grapefruit essential oil

Mix the ingredients together thoroughly and store in a sealed glass jar until needed. Use in place of your regular body moisturiser – it may be oilier than you're used to, so a little goes a long way. Give it time to soak in, too.

Lip scrub

Exfoliates the lips and makes them look fuller. Bonus: it tastes amazing! I like to make a fresh batch of this once every few weeks, but it will last for months. Just make sure you store this sweet concoction in a container with a lid otherwise the ants will find it!

1 teaspoon honey
1 teaspoon extra-virgin olive oil
1½ teaspoons brown sugar
pinch of ground allspice

Mix the ingredients together thoroughly and store in a sealed glass jar until needed. Use the tip of your finger – I use my ring finger because it's the softest – to gently apply to the lips, then rinse.

Sandy foot scrub

Brazilians have been doing this for years for smooth, beach-ready feet. As there's natural bacteria in the sand, this will only last a week if you're not using it on the beach straight after making it. But swap the sand for rock salt and it will last for ages!

2 tablespoons extra-virgin olive oil
5 drops of rosemary essential oil
2 tablespoons beach sand

Combine the oils in a small container and take it to the beach with you. Mix in the 2 tablespoons of sand then rub the lot into your feet and the dry bits of your elbows. Now go for a swim and notice how soft and silky you feel afterwards.

Floral lip balm

The clean way to condition your lips. You can use most blooms, but rose petals come up a treat. It will keep for months in little sealed jars, which make super-cute pressies too.

250 ml (1 cup) coconut oil, melted
60 g (¼ cup) beeswax
230 g (1 cup) shea butter
1 vanilla pod, split and scraped
10 g (¼ cup) rose petals (fresh or dried)

Melt the coconut oil, beeswax and shea butter in a heatproof bowl set over a saucepan of simmering water, then remove from the heat and mix through the vanilla and rose petals. While the mixture is still liquid, pour it into little glass jars. Leave to set, then enjoy. To use, gently apply to the lips with the tip of your finger.

Eye syrup

Soothes and plumps the delicate under-eye area for a youthful look. Just make sure you wash it off after applying, as it's sticky! This will keep for ages in a sealed jar.

60 ml (¼ cup) extra-virgin olive oil
1 tablespoon honey

Mix the ingredients together thoroughly (it'll be a bit gluggy at first) and store in a sealed glass jar until needed. To use, gently apply a little of the syrup around the eye sockets. It will feel a bit sticky and runny, so lie down on your back while it's on. Leave for 5 minutes then wash off. If you want to wear the eye syrup to bed, just leave out the honey – extra-virgin olive oil around the eyes is fantastic to wear to sleep.

Clay mask

Deeply cleanses and smooths the face and neck. The naturally occurring lactic acid in the yoghurt helps to tighten and tone the skin, and the honey has powerful antioxidant and antibacterial properties. If you're not using it straight away, this will keep in the fridge for a couple of days.

60 g (¼ cup) bentonite clay (a healing clay known for its ability to absorb toxins, chemicals and heavy metals – available from some health-food stores or online)
60 g (¼ cup) plain yoghurt
2 tablespoons honey

Place all of your ingredients in a bowl, mix together thoroughly, then apply the mask evenly around the face and neck (avoiding your eyes). I pop a hand towel around my shoulders, so if it gets messy it's not going all over my PJs! Leave on for a few minutes before rinsing off.

Choc, coffee and banana body scrub

This one is hard not to eat – it's so yummy! It will keep for 3 days in the fridge, though without the bananas it would last up to a year, so you can always make up a big batch without bananas and then add them to the mix when needed.

2 bananas
45 g (½ cup) ground coffee
125 ml (½ cup) coconut oil
30 g (¼ cup) raw cacao nibs

Mix the ingredients together thoroughly. Give yourself a rinse in the shower then turn the water off and scrub. Rinse off.

Summer exercise tips

When it comes to exercise, the trick is making it work for you. You've got to love it, otherwise it will feel more like a chore and it will be very hard to stick to. I enjoy yoga, running, walking, hiking, boxing and swimming in the ocean, so these are the things I do regularly. My advice is to get out into nature; you don't even realise you're exercising when there's so much to look at, and it keeps you feeling inspired and happy.

If you're just not into anything in particular then try a few things on for size. Most gyms and yoga studios will have a one- or two-week trial; use that to figure out what works for you. Personal trainers are a great investment, too. They teach you a very safe way to exercise and can put together great programs to help you achieve the goals you're after. Personal trainers *are* an investment, but they can provide that extra bit of motivation you might need.

Summer yoga

It's no secret I love a bit of yoga, and not just for the physical benefits of feeling strong – and let's be honest, a great yoga pose makes for a brill insta snap – but also for the way it makes me feel in my heart. I feel connected, grounded, clear and happy. And just like nourishing your body with good food, I think the movements and forms yoga teaches are a huge part of honouring your body. They teach self-belief, love and self-worth, which is an important message at any time of the year. The following poses are good starting points for you to build on to find the poses and sequences you love. And at the end of the day you've got to love it, otherwise you won't keep it up!

Rockstar
(Camatkarasana)
Also known as Fallen Angel or Wild Thing, this semi-backward bend opens the heart and chest and stretches the hip flexors.

Rockstar is an energising pose

Poses to energise

Great for giving you energy, lifting your mood and keeping your heart open, these poses are brilliant to do in the morning before work, and particularly good before a date (to keep your skin glowing and your heart open to receiving!).

Bridge
(*Setu Bandhasana*)
Stretches the neck, opens the chest and helps to build flexibility in the spine.

Sugarcane
(*Ardha Chandra Chapasana*)
Also known as Half Moon Bow, this pose builds endurance in the legs, opens the hips and lengthens the spine with a subtle twist and slight backwards bend.

Wheel
(*Urdhva Dhanurasana*)
Also known as Upward Bow, this pose expands the chest and shoulders, stretches the hips, core and wrist flexor muscles, and really helps to strengthen the lower back.

Poses for detoxing

Twisting poses stimulate the mid body by rinsing the organs of elimination (liver, kidneys, lungs and intestines). In yoga classes we often teach twisting poses post-Christmas and New Year to help the body cleanse and detox, and to make way for the new.

Triangle
(*Trikonasana*)
This pose really works on strengthening the core and legs. You can also feel it in your hips and it subtly opens up your rib cage as you peel your heart skyward.

Crescent Lunge
(*Anjaneyasana*)
Also known as Crescent Twist, this pose strengthens your legs and butt, opens your heart and shoulders, improves balance and core strength, and stimulates the abdominal organs.

Half Moon
(*Ardha Chandrasana*)
This is a great pose for building balance and core strength. It has also been linked to helping reduce stress hormones.

Essential ingredients

*

All oven temperatures in my recipes are for conventional ovens. If using
fan-forced, you'll need to drop the cooking temperature by 10–20°C
(check your oven manual). Wherever possible, all the foods I use in my recipes
are whole, raw, organic, seasonal, unprocessed and as close to their natural
state as possible. If you can, do the same.

Acai powder

Made from the purple berries of the acai
tree native to the Amazon rainforest, this
powder is jam-packed with antioxidants,
vitamins, calcium, iron and amino acids.
It's not very sweet straight up, so it makes
a great addition to a smoothie or an 'acai
bowl' together with lots of other fruits,
seeds and granola.

Almond butter

This ground almond paste, with all its lovely
oils, is a wonderful butter substitute. I prefer
mine raw (not roasted) because it's the
healthier option. Almonds are loaded with
fibre, good fats and protein, plus they've got
a fair bit of magnesium and calcium.

Almond meal (almond flour)

This grain-free flour is another kitchen
staple. Whole almond meal has a coarse
texture and is great in brekkie creations,
for crumbing meats and fish, and even in
desserts and raw treats. Blanched almond
meal (often called almond flour) is more
refined, as the almond skin is removed
before grinding.

Almond milk

You can add unsweetened almond milk to
pretty much any recipe that calls for milk.
You can make your own almond milk if you
have a powerful food processor. (Don't
throw away the nutty, fibrous bits: use them
to make energy balls or other raw treats.)

Amaranth

I use this Aztec seed like a grain. It's great
combined with quinoa and millet to make a
paleo granola. This is more birdseedy than
regular sugary granolas, but it is full of fibre,
minerals and vitamins.

Avocados

Avocados are a good source of fibre,
potassium and vitamin C, and although they
are high in fat, it's the good kind (unsaturated,
like olive oil). My favourite variety is Hass,
which is available all year round.

Bee pollen

Bee pollen is the soft yellow 'dust' from
flowers that bees brush into the pollen sacs
on their back legs. It's very high in protein
and nutrients. People with pollen allergies
should avoid bee pollen; vegans might prefer
to leave it out, too. I sprinkle it on pancakes,
muesli, porridge and smoothies.

Black peppercorns

I reckon freshly ground black peppercorns taste loads better than the pre-ground stuff. If a recipe calls for a more subtle taste of black pepper, I just grind it more with my mortar and pestle.

Buckwheat

Despite its name, buckwheat is not a grain but the fruit of a plant related to sorrel and rhubarb. It's sold as groats or flour. Groats are the light-coloured kernels that you can buy whole or ground (cracked) and either raw or roasted (called kasha). Buckwheat flour is available in light and dark versions. The darker type contains more of the hull, therefore more fibre and nutrients, and has a stronger, nuttier flavour. I love to use buckwheat groats for porridge or as a replacement for burghul (cracked wheat) in tabouli. Buckwheat flour makes delicious pancakes and slices, and I often add it to gluten-free recipes.

Cacao

Technically, cacao and cocoa are the same thing, but in everyday use, cacao usually refers to the raw, unprocessed beans, and cocoa to the beans that have been roasted and processed (and usually combined with milk and sugar to make chocolate). Raw cacao powder is the healthiest way to get a chocolate hit; add it to a smoothie, or make hot chocolate, energy balls or a raw choccy cake. It's delicious and full of health benefits, especially for our brains. It's high in magnesium (great for our muscles and heart) and phenylalanine, a precursor to two brain chemicals that make us feel good (norepinephrine and dopamine) – maybe that's why we love chocolate so much!

Carob powder

Carob powder is delicious, with a sweet, chocolate-like taste. It's a great source of fibre and minerals including calcium and magnesium. It's also great for digestion and was traditionally used for settling upset stomachs. Sometimes I use it instead of cacao in my smoothies when I want my chocolate flavour nice and subtle, and when I don't want to be shaken up by the stimulants (caffeine and theobromine) that are found in regular cacao. Carob is an acquired taste but personally, I love the stuff!

Chia seeds

Chia seeds provide an amazing hit of nutrients, especially protein, calcium and omega-3 fatty acids. To get the full benefits, soak the seeds – even five minutes is enough. They're quite gelatinous, so people use them to thicken sauces and as a substitute for eggs. I add them to my brekkie every day, and sprinkle them on smoothies and salads. Don't boil or bake them at high temperatures as this will reduce their nutrients.

Chilli

Chillies speed up your metabolic rate (good for weight control), promote heart health, and are full of antioxidants (great for your skin). I slice them up fresh to have in salads and veggie dishes or to season meat, and sometimes I even add a tiny pinch of flakes to smoothies, slices and cakes. The mildest chilli is the longish, thin cayenne chilli (it comes in red, green and yellow), followed by the medium–hot ball chilli, the hot jalapeño, the very hot, tiny bird's eye chilli and the scorching habanero.

Coconut, dried

You can get desiccated, that's super-fine; shredded, which is long, thin pieces; and flaked, which is chunky and chewy. I love them all, and you'll find them throughout my recipes.

Coconut flour

Coconut flour is quite dense and needs help sticking together, so if I'm making coconut-flour pancakes, for example, I will add an extra egg to help bind the mixture. But it tastes brill!

Coconut milk and coconut cream

These are great for curries, pancake mixes, porridge and smoothies. Coconut milk and cream are made the same way, just using different amounts of water. You can make them yourself or buy them ready-made. If possible, buy organic coconut milk and cream packed in BPA-free tins (BPA is a toxic chemical that works like oestrogen and can affect your hormones).

Coconut nectar

This has a slightly stronger flavour than honey or even agave – almost like a mild molasses. It's loaded with minerals and contains less fructose than agave and honey, too. But remember, it's still a sweetener, so use it in moderation.

Coconut oil

Coconut oil is solid at cooler temperatures. Unlike regular olive oil (not extra-virgin), coconut oil doesn't break down or go rancid when cooked at high temperatures – making it a winner. People worry about coconut oil

making them fat. It *is* a saturated fat, but it's a medium-chain fatty acid, which means the body can use it quickly (rather than having to store it). It's awesome used topically, too – I use it to moisturise my face and body. It's also thermogenic, meaning it helps to speed up your metabolism.

Coconut sugar

Also known as coconut sap sugar or coconut palm sugar, this is coconut nectar that has been dried. Its granulated texture makes it easy to use in place of raw sugar in baking. It has a delicious molasses flavour.

Coconut water

Coconut water is the liquid from young coconuts – a bit like Mother Nature's very own electrolyte drink. It's naturally sweet. It makes a fantastic base for smoothies and, if you're a cocktail fan, then it's great mixed with your favourite alcohol (and the electrolytes will help to prevent a hangover!).

Dates, medjool

Dates are a great source of the electrolyte potassium, which is a key player for heart health. Plus, they're full of fibre and will keep you regular. Medjool dates are bigger, sweeter and squidgier than regular dried dates. They're very sweet, though, so to avoid a sugar rush when snacking on them I pop the seed out and replace it with a brazil nut. The protein and fat from the nut help to lower the glycaemic load and make for a slower release of energy.

Dulse flakes

I like to sprinkle this dried seaweed over salads. It's a really great source of iodine, but if you get too heavy handed it can taste pretty full on, so keep it to a sprinkle.

Eggs

I always choose organic and free-range eggs, because they taste unreal and because the chickens have access to pasture and sunlight, and generally have a much better life than caged hens.

Goji berries

These berries are a great source of antioxidants and have a nice flavour (they're not too sweet, more like a sourish sultana). You can add them to any dish (sweet or savoury): sprinkle them on your brekkie or salads, use them in a raw nut mix, or even in your tea.

Herbs and spices

Fresh herbs and spices are the key to adding flavour to your food creations, not to mention the antioxidant hit you'll reap from them. Some of my favourites are cinnamon, nutmeg, paprika, chilli flakes, cumin, coriander, cardamom, fennel, dill, rosemary . . . wow, the list goes on!

Honey, raw

Raw honey has been filtered, but in a way that doesn't destroy its nutrients. It is not pasteurised (the heating and filtration process that makes it clear), so all its beneficial enzymes are still present. Raw honey can be solid at room temperature (depending on how cold it is), and is milky

(not clear). It's about twice as sweet as sugar, so you don't need to use as much. Plus, local honey is now a big thing as more and more people are setting up 'rooftop' hives, which means the bees will be feeding off local pollens – having locally made honey can help decrease the symptoms of hay fever, so it's a great option.

Lavender

Lavender is a sweet herb native to Northern Africa and the mountains of the Mediterranean. When you think of lavender you might think of beauty products and soaps, but it's actually so much more than that – with its anti-inflammatory and antiseptic qualities it's also used to treat wounds topically, and the bit I love is that it helps to calm the nervous system, easing insomnia, depression and anxiety. I like to pop a few sprigs on my pillow for a good night's sleep.

LSA

LSA stands for (ground) linseed, sunflower seed and almond, and it's an awesome superfood. It's high in fibre, good fats and veggo protein, plus it has a nice hit of B vitamins. I use it in smoothies, raw creations, breakfast combos and on top of salads. I don't cook or bake with LSA as the linseed and sunflower seeds lose their nutritional benefits when heated.

Macadamia nuts and oil

Macadamia nuts are an excellent source of mono-unsaturated fats and a top brain food. I love their texture and flavour and use them in brekkies, smoothies, salads and baking. Macadamia oil is so pure I even use it on my skin.

Maple syrup

Maple syrup is a wonderful sweetener: it has a great flavour, is full of minerals and has less fructose than honey, dates and agave. Make sure you choose 100 per cent syrup, not the imitation stuff. It costs more, but it's so much healthier.

Millet

This is an ancient seed that we use like a grain. It's gluten-free so great for any paleo recipe. Rinse millet before using. I love to add a little to a mash to give it more depth, use it to make a creamy coconut porridge, and just cook it up the same way I would rice or quinoa.

Monk fruit

Also known as luo han guo, this is a small, round fruit grown in Southeast Asia. It's around 150–200 times sweeter than sugar and contains zero calories, so is much like stevia but without the aftertaste that stevia has. I buy it in liquid form.

Nut milks

You can whip up your own nut milks easily; all you need is a handful of raw nuts (always use raw for nut milks), a couple of cups of water and a good blender – then whizz it up. Sometimes I add nutmeg and cinnamon so it's like a nut-milk chai. And you can either keep the pulp in (it's full of fibre) or strain it with a nut-milk bag or muslin cloth, then use that pulp to make a raw treat the next day.

Nuts and seeds

Nuts and seeds are brilliant sources of good fats. When my recipes refer to activating

nuts, this means to soak them in water for 2–3 hours (or overnight if possible) then rinse. This removes enzyme inhibitors and makes them easier to digest. After rinsing (unless you're about to blend them up for a smoothie or raw treat), spread the nuts out on a baking tray and place in a 50°C oven or dehydrator to dry out (this will take anywhere from 6 to 24 hours depending on the type of nut). Store your activated nuts in sealed glass jars in the pantry.

Oats

Pure oats don't contain gluten, but because of the way we process them, most oatmeal brands have been cross-contaminated with minuscule amounts of wheat, barley and/ or rye, so we can't call them 'gluten-free'. About 30 per cent of people who have coeliac disease cannot tolerate oats (even when the cross-contamination is almost eliminated), so if you have coeliac disease, or a particularly severe gluten allergy, proceed with caution.

Olive oil, extra-virgin

Olive oil is a great source of mono-unsaturated fat. Regular olive oil becomes unstable and rancid when used in cooking at high temperatures, but I was jazzed to discover recently that good-quality extra-virgin varieties are much higher in polyphenols (that's the antioxidant part of the olive oil) and this prevents the double bond in the mono-unsaturated fat from breaking. Just make sure the oil you buy is extra-virgin, which means it's been pressed once, with no chemicals or additives. And good quality, of course, if you're going to cook with it.

Pomegranate

Pomegranate seeds are packed with antioxidants. I have them fresh in salads. Dried seeds are also yummy in salads and trail mixes and as smoothie toppers. The juice is great, but make sure you get the 100 per cent pure juice.

Pumpkin seeds

Also known as pepitas, pumpkin seeds are full of zinc, an important mineral for health. Zinc is found in every cell of our body and plays a big role in immunity, cell division, cell growth, wound healing and the breakdown of carbs.

Quinoa

This seed is packed with nutrients and is very high in protein, so it's excellent if you're vegetarian or vegan. It's also versatile: you can get quinoa seeds, quinoa flakes, puffed quinoa, and even quinoa milk and quinoa flour. There is white quinoa, red and a royal black, though they're pretty much on par nutrient-wise (the coloured ones may have a slightly higher mineral content). I find the white has the mildest flavour. You cook it in a similar way to rice and it suits both sweet and savoury dishes. You can use the flakes to make a porridge for brekkie, the seeds as the base of a superfood salad for lunch or with curry for dinner, and the flour for making cakes, muffins and pancakes.

Rice malt syrup

A carbohydrate blend of glucose and maltose, rice malt syrup is a good sweetener alternative for those who have difficulty absorbing fructose. Made from cooked fermented rice, it is a relatively slow-release sweetener, which means it won't put as much of a load on the liver as pure glucose does and will be less likely to give you that sugar 'spike' that leads to soaring and crashing energy levels.

Salt

I love to use pink salt in my cooking. It tastes just like normal salt but has loads more minerals (about 84 trace minerals, in fact). It's great to use in place of regular table salt and looks so pretty. I use Murray River or Himalayan. Celtic salt and rock salt are healthy options, too. Use salt sparingly, though, and stay away from the bleached stuff.

Spirulina powder

Spirulina powder is extracted from algae and contains a super-rich source of proteins, vitamins, minerals, essential fatty acids and antioxidants. I like to add it to my smoothies for an extra energy and nutrient boost.

Stevia

Stevia, which is made from the leaves of a South American herb, is about 300 times sweeter than sugar and has no calories and no impact on blood sugar levels. You can buy it in powder form or as a liquid. Use it sparingly – if you use more than a couple of drops of liquid you'll get a pretty nasty aftertaste. It doesn't taste quite the same as sugar, but once you're used to it, you'll be converted.

Tahini

Tahini is a paste made from crushed sesame seeds. You can buy hulled (where the seed casing has been removed) and unhulled (made from the whole seed). Both are high in protein and good fats. Hulled tahini is lighter in colour and has a milder taste; unhulled has more calcium and fibre. You can also get black tahini, which tastes similar to hulled tahini. Tahini is great in salad dressings, dips and energy balls.

Tamari

Tamari is a Japanese fermented soy sauce with a darker colour and richer flavour than traditional soy sauce. It contains much less salt and is a good source of vitamin B3, protein and manganese. It's made with far less wheat than normal soy sauce, if any, and is therefore a good low-gluten or gluten-free alternative. Look for 'gluten free' on the label.

Tea

I love herbal teas, as they're an ace way to add a whole lot of nutritional value to your diet. They can be as simple as adding a knob of ginger to a cup of hot water or as intriguing as blossoming flowers. I love Brahmi (an ancient Indian herb used in Ayurvedic medicine) for brain power, lavender for calming the nervous system, chamomile for digestion and thyme for the immune system.

Vanilla pods

Vanilla pods, like honey and cinnamon, are a great libido enhancer. Wrap the pods in foil, seal them in a zip-lock bag, and store them in a cool, dark place so they don't dry out. Vanilla pods can be pricey, but you can always use powdered vanilla (make sure it's 100 per cent vanilla) or vanilla extract (not the chemically produced essence) instead.

Xanthan gum

Xanthan gum is a natural ingredient produced by fermentation of glucose or sucrose. It's great for gluten-free baking, helping to give your homemade goodies a lovely crumb and reduce crumbling.

Yoghurt

Some people who react badly to cow's milk can tolerate yoghurt as it's partially fermented and is a little easier to digest. Choose organic or biodynamic full-cream options, as they're more nutritious than low-fat yoghurt. If you can't handle cow's milk yoghurt, try sheep's or goat's milk yoghurt – they have a slightly stronger flavour. Then there are coconut or nut milk yoghurts for a vegan option. Always read the label carefully; you don't want any added sugar or gelatine. We're after real foods, as close to their natural state as possible.

Brekkies
to kickstart
your day

Happiness fruit salad

＊

The name says it all! Think about it: when you eat something this bright it just makes you want to smile. I think that happiness plays a huge part in our health, so when you sit down to have this meal think about one thing you're grateful for then smile and enjoy. The addition of avo might sound weird, but trust me, it adds the best creaminess to the salad, not to mention good fats to make your skin glow!

1 large papaya, peeled and cut into chunks

1 punnet (125 g) blueberries

1 punnet (250 g) strawberries, halved

1 punnet (125 g) raspberries

1 avocado, sliced

½ bunch of mint, leaves picked and shredded

zest, juice and flesh of 1 lime

2 tablespoons chia seeds

edible flowers, to serve (optional)

Place all the ingredients in a large bowl and gently toss together. Munch immediately, or store in a sealed container for up to 1 day.

Serves 4

TIP
When you are selecting a papaya, make sure it's ripe (you can tell by the smell — it will have a sweetish smell with a hint of dirty socks!).

Wishing granola

Although ancient seeds like quinoa, amaranth and millet may be new to many of us, these guys have been around for ages and are full of fibre – quinoa is also a great source of veggo protein. I love the texture they bring to this granola. The reason this is called wishing granola is because I believe the energy you put into food affects not only the way it tastes but also the effect it has on you. So when you make this recipe, set a little wish – it can be a goal or affirmation – into the creation too and watch the magic unfold. Only you need to know the wish, but it should come from a place of pure intention.

150 g (1 cup) quinoa flakes

150 g (1 cup) amaranth flakes

200 g (1 cup) rolled millet

60 g (½ cup) chopped walnuts, activated if possible (see page 35)

70 g (½ cup) chopped macadamia nuts, activated if possible (see page 35)

30 g (¼ cup) goji berries

60 g (½ cup) dried white mulberries

1 vanilla pod, split and scraped

¼ teaspoon ground cinnamon

60 ml (¼ cup) coconut oil, melted

60 ml (¼ cup) maple syrup

pinch of salt flakes

Preheat the oven to 180°C and line a baking tray with baking paper.

In a large mixing bowl, combine all the ingredients and mix well. Spoon the mixture evenly into the tray and bake for 20–25 minutes, or until golden brown on top.

Allow to cool before crumbling the mixture into clumps.

Store in an airtight container in the pantry. Enjoy it for brekkie with almond milk, fresh berries and banana.

Serves 6

TIP
Used as a topping for
coconut yoghurt this
makes a lovely night-time
treat too!

Lamington granola

❋

I love making healthy brekkies that taste as good as treats, and this paleo lamington granola is the perfect example. The nuts are an excellent source of mono-unsaturated fats, great for getting the brain into gear and keeping your skin clear and glowing. Ah, my dream brekkie – especially with my raspberry–chia jam.

100 g (⅔ cup) almonds, roughly chopped, activated if possible (see page 35)

50 g (½ cup) walnuts, activated if possible (see page 35), roughly chopped

60 g (½ cup) sunflower seeds

50 g (⅓ cup) pumpkin seeds

60 ml (¼ cup) maple syrup (or rice malt syrup)

30 g (¼ cup) raw cacao nibs

60 g (1 cup) shredded coconut

1 vanilla pod, split and scraped

60 g (½ cup) dried white mulberries (or dried cranberries)

30 g (¼ cup) raw cacao powder

60 ml (¼ cup) coconut oil, melted

pinch of salt flakes

Raspberry–chia jam

375 g (3 cups) raspberries, fresh or frozen

50 g (¼ cup) coconut sugar

30 g (¼ cup) chia seeds

1 vanilla pod, split and scraped

Toppings

coconut yoghurt

chocolate almond milk (just blitz up almond milk with ½ teaspoon raw cacao powder and add a drop of stevia if it needs sweetening)

fresh raspberries

Preheat the oven to 180°C.

Combine all of the granola ingredients (except the chia jam and toppings) in one big bowl – you want the mixture to feel quite 'sticky' – then spread it evenly onto a lined baking tray. Bring the heat down to 140°C and bake for 45–50 minutes, until the mixture is crunchy and the house smells like sweet coconut chocolate (or lamingtons!).

While the granola is baking, get cracking on the chia jam. Combine the raspberries and coconut sugar in a small saucepan and cook over a medium heat until the berries soften. Add the chia seeds and heat gently until nicely thickened – this will take about 10 minutes. Stir through the vanilla seeds, then remove from the heat and leave to cool. Store in the fridge for up to 7 days.

I love to have my first bowl of granola warm from the oven with the raspberry–chia jam and some coconut yoghurt, chocolate almond milk and fresh berries. The rest will keep for weeks in an airtight jar in the pantry, but I make a batch weekly as it goes so fast!

Serves 6–8

TIP
If you don't have a vanilla
pod to hand, just use
¼ teaspoon of pure
powdered vanilla.

Tropicana chia pud

This one is very simple to make and you can mix and match the fruit to suit your tastebuds. I do love how pretty these creations are. If you want to take things to the next level and add a touch of mystical fairy magic, think about topping these puds with edible flowers. The chia seeds in these little beauties deliver a whole whack of nutrients, including protein, calcium and omega-3 fatty acids.

60 g (½ cup) chia seeds

250 ml (1 cup) coconut milk

2 tablespoons shredded coconut, plus extra to serve

½ vanilla pod, split and scraped

2 tablespoons maple syrup, plus extra to serve (optional)

1 large mango, cut into cubes

zest and juice of ½ lime

fresh edible flowers, to serve (optional)

Place the chia seeds, coconut milk, shredded coconut, vanilla seeds and maple syrup in a bowl or jar and give them a good mix. Cover or seal and pop in the fridge overnight.

In the morning, divide your pudding among 3 small or 2 large serving bowls. Top with freshly cut cubes of mango, lime juice, lime zest and shredded coconut. If it's not quite sweet enough, by all means give it another drizzle of maple syrup. Decorate with edible flowers if you like.

Serves 2–3

Coconut–berry (almost) ice cream

I like to make this one for brekkie, even though it's pretty much an ice cream. One of the reasons I love popping berries into this dish is because they provide the body with a huge hit of the antioxidants needed to help combat free radical damage and prevent skin ageing. Couple that with the coconut cream, which is a brilliant source of the fats that the skin needs to thrive, and you're off to a great start!

310 g (2 cups) frozen blueberries

250 ml (1 cup) coconut cream, chilled

6 fresh strawberries, hulled and sliced into discs (I think they look pretty in discs but you can chop them any way you like)

30 g (½ cup) shredded coconut

mint leaves, to serve (optional)

Pour your frozen berries into a blender with the coconut cream and whizz together until smooth. Then pour into two bowls and top with the strawberries, shredded coconut and some fresh mint, if you like. (I tear the big mint leaves but leave the little ones whole.) It's that easy. This makes an ace super-fresh brekkie but it's also a good night-time treat. Eat straight away or store in the freezer for an hour before enjoying.

Serves 2

TIPS
If you want to tweak this recipe, add the juice of half a lime for a little extra flavour.
And if you can't get your hands on frozen blueberries then any old
frozen berry will work – I also love it with blackberries.

The perfect Hawaiian acai bowl

This is my go-to summer brekkie. It works well as a smoothie too – all you have to do is add a smidge more coconut water. It's no secret that I'm in love with Hawaii and the acai bowls they make there are the inspiration for this creation. Acai powder is full of antioxidants, vitamins, calcium, iron and amino acids. It's not very sweet on its own – in fact, I reckon it tastes a bit like olives – but is perfect whizzed together with a whole heap of other goodies like this.

155 g (1 cup) frozen blueberries

1 frozen banana (peel it before you freeze it)

1 tablespoon unsweetened acai powder

250 ml (1 cup) coconut water

30 g (¼ cup) chia seeds

To serve

fresh kiwifruit, cut into discs

fresh banana, cut into discs

sprinkle of Wishing Granola or Lamington Granola (see pages 42 and 44)

raw honey (or maple syrup)

Pop the berries, banana, acai powder, coconut water and chia seeds into a blender and whizz everything up. You might need to give it a few pulses to get the right consistency. Then pour the mixture into sweet little bowls (or two halves of a coconut if you're feeling extra tropical!) and top with fresh kiwi, banana, granola and a dash of honey. Hello Hawaiian magic.

Serves 2

Double chocolate brownie smoothie bowl

✳

I love it when I can have a treat without beating myself up about it, and this one ticks all the right boxes – it's super clean, raw, vegan and healthy. The cacao powder will get your brain buzzing and give you that lovely chocolate hit you're after in the healthiest way. In fact, chocolate contains the same chemicals that we release when we fall in love, so maybe that's why we love it so much!

1 avocado

2 frozen bananas (peel them before you freeze them)

2 tablespoons raw cacao powder

2 tablespoons maple syrup (or sweetener of your choice)

Topping

1 teaspoon raw cacao nibs

1 tablespoon crushed walnuts, activated if possible (see page 35)

1 teaspoon bee pollen (optional)

edible flowers (optional)

Pop the avocado, bananas, cacao powder and maple syrup in a blender and process until super smooth. Pulse a couple of times to make sure you process any last little chunks of avo.

Combine the topping ingredients in a separate small bowl. Pour the smoothie into serving glasses or bowls and sprinkle over the topping.

Serves 2

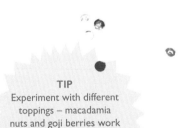

TIP
Experiment with different toppings – macadamia nuts and goji berries work well, or even just a sprinkle of shredded or desiccated coconut.

Chilli egg wrap

I love chillies and they are said to not only boost your metabolism but also be quite addictive – you can build up a tolerance to them and need more and more of them to get that kick you're after. I know I'm addicted!

knob of butter

1 tablespoon extra-virgin olive oil

4 eggs, whisked

1 capsicum, diced (I use red)

½ teaspoon chilli flakes, plus extra to serve (optional)

6 cherry tomatoes, quartered

pinch of paprika

salt flakes and freshly ground black pepper

1 avocado, sliced

a few coriander sprigs, leaves picked

squeeze of lime juice

chilli flakes, to serve

Gluten-free wraps

130 g (1 cup) buckwheat flour, sifted

pinch of salt flakes

250 ml (1 cup) almond milk

1 egg, beaten

1 tablespoon coconut oil or a knob of butter

To make the wraps, place the sifted flour and salt in a large bowl. Make a small well in the middle, add the almond milk slowly and start to fold it through the mixture with a wooden spoon, then add the egg and mix well until you have a smooth batter.

Heat the coconut oil or butter in a large frying pan over a medium heat. Pour in half of the mixture and immediately tilt the pan around to spread the mixture to the edge to form a thin, crepe-like wrap. Use the back of a spatula to smooth the mixture out evenly – the thinner the wrap the easier it is to flip! Once the wrap starts to bubble in the middle and curl at the edge (about a minute or two), carefully flip and cook for another minute or two on the other side. Cover and keep warm while you repeat the process with the remaining batter.

Pop your butter and olive oil into a saucepan over a medium heat, add the egg, capsicum, chilli, tomatoes, paprika and salt and pepper, then just move them about in the pan until you have a nice scramble. Turn the heat off.

Spoon your mixture onto the wraps, add the sliced avo and coriander, then a squeeze of fresh lime juice and a sprinkling of chilli flakes. Roll up and enjoy!

Serves 2

Super scramble

I love starting the day with this much nutrition, though to be honest I've made this one for lunch and dinner at times too! Remember, if there's an ingredient listed here that you don't like or can't get, you can always sub it with something you love – like asparagus in place of broccoli, or sometimes I forget to buy capsicums so I just add a bit of cauliflower instead. It's about making it work for you. When I make it for Dad I hold the chillies, but when it's for me I add double!

1 teaspoon coconut oil

1 red chilli, finely sliced

½ small red onion, sliced

½ red capsicum, diced

70 g (1 cup) finely sliced kale

handful of baby spinach

60 g (1 cup) broccoli florets

4 eggs

salt flakes and freshly ground black pepper

2 tablespoons chopped fresh herbs

Melt the coconut oil in a frying pan over a medium–high heat. Add the chilli, onion, capsicum, kale, spinach and broccoli and sauté until tender.

Whisk the eggs together with a little salt and pepper in a bowl and add to the vegetable mixture, stirring constantly. When the egg mixture is almost set, remove from the heat and turn onto a plate (the eggs will continue to cook with the residual heat). Sprinkle with the chopped herbs, divide into two equal portions and serve immediately.

Serves 2

TIP
If you can't get your hands on baby spinach, go for anything green; kale, mustard greens, silverbeet, English spinach or even beetroot tops work really well.

Zucchini fritters and poached eggs with cashew and lime aioli

Zucchini fritters are awesome! I love the flavour and texture they bring to a meal, and with the added protein of the poached eggs this is the perfect way to kickstart your day.

4 large zucchini, grated

2 teaspoons salt

30 g (¼ cup) coconut flour

2 eggs

pinch of freshly ground black pepper

pinch of cayenne pepper

60 ml (¼ cup) extra-virgin olive oil, plus extra to serve

mint leaves, to serve

Cashew and lime aioli

80 g (½ cup) cashew nuts, activated if possible (see page 35)

2 tablespoons extra-virgin olive oil

zest and juice of 1 lime

2 garlic cloves

pinch of salt flakes

up to 125 ml (½ cup) almond milk, to thin, if needed

Poached eggs

splash of apple cider vinegar

2 eggs

It's important to get all the moisture out of the grated zucchini, so tip it into a bowl, sprinkle it with the salt and let it sit for 10 minutes. Then pick up the zucchini in handfuls and squeeze as much liquid out of it as you can (I do this over the sink).

Place the squeezed zucchini in a clean bowl. Add the coconut flour, eggs, pepper and cayenne and give it a good mix.

Heat the olive oil in a pan over medium heat. Grab little handfuls of the mixture – about ¼ cup in volume – and shape them into fritters, then pop them into the pan and cook for about 3 minutes. When they're starting to turn golden underneath, flip and cook them for another 2 minutes on the other side. I can usually cook about four at a time, but if you're cooking in batches then make sure to add a little more oil between each batch.

Meanwhile, whip up the aioli. Pop the cashews into a powerful blender or food processer with the olive oil, lime juice and zest, garlic and salt. I love my aioli thick, so this recipe makes it really paste-like. If you prefer it runnier, add almond milk until you get the consistency you like.

Keep the fritters warm while you poach your eggs. Fill a saucepan with water to a depth of 10 cm and add the vinegar (this helps prevent the egg white from spreading). Pop on the lid and bring to the boil over a high heat. Crack one egg – it's best to do one at a time – into a cup.

When the water is boiling, remove the lid and reduce the heat to medium. Grab a spoon and carefully swirl the water to create a little whirlpool, then slide the egg into the centre of the whirlpool, holding the cup close to the water. Cook the egg for 3–4 minutes – for a soft yolk – then remove it with a slotted spoon. Repeat with the remaining egg.

To serve, divide the fritters between two plates, add a mega dollop of the aioli and top each with a poached egg. Finish with a drizzle of olive oil and a sprinkling of mint leaves.

Serves 2 (makes 4–5 fritters)

Simple snacking
made easy

TIP
If you don't like
pecans, replace them
with your favo nut –
just make sure it's raw.

Aussie super balls

❋

Before you knock the fact that prunes are the first ingredient and you think they're pretty much just used to make you regular, know this; they are native to Australia and sit higher on the ORAC scale — that's the scale that measures the level of antioxidants in foods — than blueberries and goji berries. So they're pretty awesome for us, plus they're cheap as chips here in Australia, so try using them in some of your recipe creations.

220 g (1 cup) pitted soft prunes, chopped

120 g (1 cup) finely chopped pecans, activated if possible (see page 35)

30 g (¼ cup) goji berries

30 g (¼ cup) raw cacao powder

¼ teaspoon ground cinnamon

pinch of salt flakes

45 g (½ cup) desiccated coconut

Combine the chopped prunes, pecans, goji berries, cacao, cinnamon and salt in a bowl and mix well. Roll the mixture into little balls and roll on a plate of desiccated coconut to coat them.

These last for weeks in a sealed container in the fridge, but I'm sure they'll get gobbled up sooner than that. Plus, they make great pressies!

Makes about 30 balls

Happy hearts trail mix

I love being organised when it comes to food; it helps keep me on track. This trail mix is perfect for when you feel like something just a little bit sweet. The goji berries are a great source of antioxidants and have a lovely, slightly sourish flavour that works so well with the macas and all the other yummy bits and pieces in here.

80 g (½ cup) macadamia nuts, activated if possible (see page 35)

30 g (½ cup) shredded coconut

30 g (¼ cup) raw cacao nibs

60 g (½ cup) goji berries

80 g (½ cup) almonds, activated if possible (see page 35)

30 g (¼ cup) pumpkin seeds

30 g (¼ cup) dried cranberries

Place everything in a bowl and mix well. Store in an airtight container in the pantry, or divide among six little containers ready for snacks on the go!

Makes 6 serves

High-protein berry seedy granola bars

These bars are all about upping the natural proteins with seeds. I love to make a big batch of them on the weekend so that I'm set for snacks for the week ahead.

200 g (1 cup) buckwheat groats

35 g (⅓ cup) rolled oats

50 g (⅓ cup) pumpkin seeds

40 g (⅓ cup) sunflower seeds

20 g (⅓ cup) shredded coconut

50 g (⅓ cup) dried blueberries

30 g (¼ cup) dried cranberries

30 g (¼ cup) raisins

80 ml (⅓ cup) rice malt syrup

80 ml (⅓ cup) coconut oil, melted

160 g (⅔ cup) almond butter

1 teaspoon ground cinnamon

pinch of ground nutmeg

pinch of salt flakes

Preheat the oven to 180°C and line a 27 cm x 18 cm baking tray with baking paper.

Mix all the ingredients together thoroughly in a large bowl. (I love using my hands as they do a better job than any spoon, and it feels like I'm adding a little bit of extra love to the recipe.) Spoon the mixture into the baking tray and press evenly over the base. Bake for 30–35 minutes, or until golden brown.

Allow to cool for 30 minutes in the fridge before carefully cutting into chunky bars. Store in an airtight container in the fridge and enjoy all week long for brekkie or snacks.

Makes 12–14 bars

TIP
This recipe works really well with macadamia nuts and walnuts, too, but I reckon it would work with pretty much any nut. Try it with almonds, brazil nuts, hazelnuts, pistachios ... the list goes on.

Maple pecans

These should come with a warning! I honestly have to give these away when I make them, otherwise I'll eat them all in one go. They do make an unreal gift. You can always tweak the spices to work for your tastebuds — my dad isn't a ginger fan, so I'll hold the ginger if I'm making these for him. They work really well with allspice too. The maple syrup helps hold everything together and has a great flavour, as well as being full of beneficial minerals like manganese and zinc.

170 ml (⅔ cup) maple syrup

2 tablespoons coconut oil

½ teaspoon ground cinnamon

½ teaspoon ground nutmeg

¼ teaspoon ground ginger

pinch of salt flakes

400 g (4 cups) pecans, activated if possible (see page 35)

2 tablespoons shredded coconut

Line a baking tray with baking paper.

Heat the maple syrup, coconut oil, spices and salt in a large saucepan over a medium heat. When the mixture starts to bubble, add the nuts, coconut and 1 tablespoon of water. Cook, uncovered, for 5–7 minutes, or until the liquid evaporates, stirring constantly so the nuts are covered and the maple coating doesn't burn.

Spread the nuts in an even layer on the prepared tray and leave to cool and harden (about 20 minutes). Then dive on them (that's what I usually do)! Store in an airtight container in the pantry for up to 6 months.

Makes about 400 g (4 cups)

Crispy kale chippies

This recipe is brilliant because you can have the kale chippies on their own or – as I like to do – you can crumble them up and pop them on top of a salad. They add a great texture and a punch of flavour, not to mention being a top source of magnesium, fibre, iron, vitamin K and calcium. I call kale the king of leafy greens and try to add it to just about anything.

750 g kale (about 2 large bunches), stalks removed, leaves cut into rough chunks

1 teaspoon paprika

1 teaspoon chilli flakes

2 tablespoons extra-virgin olive oil

salt flakes and freshly ground black pepper

Preheat the oven to 180°C.

Line two or three large baking trays with baking paper and scatter the kale over them in a single layer. Sprinkle with paprika and chilli flakes, drizzle over the olive oil and season to taste with salt and pepper. Bake for 10 minutes. You won't believe how light and crispy they are! Store leftovers – if you've got any – in an airtight container.

Serves 4–6

TIP
The quantity of kale used here is about two big bunches, but by the time you remove the stalks and bake it, it won't seem so huge (kale shrinks heaps during cooking). You can make all kinds of flavour variations — sometimes I pop macadamia nuts, cashews, a little olive oil and curry spices in the blender and rub that all over the kale chippies before baking.

Perfect paleo bread

Paleo bread is a staple in my house. I like to make a loaf, slice it up and freeze it – then there's always some on hand to have with eggs or avo, and it works really well with sweet things like almond butter and maple syrup, too. This paleo bread tastes better than regular bread, I reckon!

500 g (4 cups) grated pumpkin (Jap or butternut work well)

pinch of salt flakes

2 teaspoons gluten-free baking powder

300 g (3 cups) almond meal (or hazelnut meal)

125 ml (½ cup) extra-virgin olive oil

2 eggs

30 g (¼ cup) pumpkin seeds

Preheat the oven to 180°C and line a 20 cm loaf tin with baking paper (or the nearest size you have to that – it will still work out).

Place the grated pumpkin, salt and baking powder in a bowl, add the almond meal and mix really well. Then in goes the olive oil and eggs. Combine everything really well – look out for any lumps of almond or hazelnut meal.

When it's completely mixed, spoon the dough into the loaf tin then sprinkle with the pumpkin seeds. Bake for 1 hour, then check. If you insert a skewer and it comes out clean, it's cooked. It can take up to an hour and a half in some ovens, so don't sweat if it needs a little longer.

When the bread is cooked, remove it from the oven and let it cool in the tin for about 45 minutes (though I love it hot!). Then slice off a piece and get cracking. Delishimo!

Makes 1 loaf

Metabolism-boosting quinoa wraps

This is my go-to recipe when I know I'm going to be travelling – I'll make a big batch so I've got healthy plane snacks. Nori is a brilliant source of iodine, which we need for healthy thyroid function – our thyroid is in charge of regulating our metabolism.

400 g (2 cups) quinoa, any colour (I love red)

2 long red chillies, finely diced

60 g (2 cups) coriander leaves, finely chopped

150 g (1 cup) cherry tomatoes, halved

50 g (1 cup) baby spinach

zest and juice of 1 lime

60 ml (¼ cup) extra-virgin olive oil

salt flakes and freshly ground black pepper

8 nori seaweed sheets

2 large avocados, sliced into thin strips

Place the quinoa in a saucepan with 1 litre of water. Bring it to the boil and simmer, covered, for 10–15 minutes until all the water is absorbed and the quinoa is fluffy (it will have tripled in size and appear to have sprouted little 'tails'). Remove from the heat and transfer to a large mixing bowl. Add the chilli, coriander, cherry tomatoes and spinach and mix well. Add the lime juice and zest, olive oil and salt and pepper to taste, and give it another toss. Divide it into eight even portions in the bowl.

Place the first nori sheet on a cutting board or rolling mat (or just a clean surface).

Place a few slices of avocado along the lower part of the nori sheet, then spoon one portion of the quinoa mixture in a sausage-like shape along the lower edge of the nori sheet (closest to you). Moisten the top edge with a pastry brush dipped in water. Now gently roll the sheet up away from you. The trick is you want to roll it tightly, so that it holds everything in – trust me I've learnt this one the hard way. The moistened top edge should be like a little envelope flap, sealing it up.

Repeat with the remaining sheets, avo and quinoa mixture until you have eight wraps. You can serve these whole or slice them up. Munch on some right away!

Makes 8 wraps

TIP
Leftovers make great
lunches for work.
They will last for
2 days stored in a
sealed container in
the fridge.

Roasted sweet spud with avo, pecans and tahini dressing

I like to use hulled tahini for this recipe – where the outer husks of the sesame seeds have been taken off before grinding – as the phytic acid which otherwise makes these seeds a little hard to digest has been removed. Also, remember not to peel your sweet spuds – there are loads of antioxidants in the skin.

2 sweet potatoes, cut into 1 cm slices

1 teaspoon ground cumin

1 teaspoon ground cinnamon

60 g (½ cup) pecans, activated if possible (see page 35)

2 tablespoons extra-virgin olive oil, plus extra to serve

2 tablespoons maple syrup

salt flakes and freshly ground black pepper

sprinkle of paprika, to serve

Herbed avo mash

2 large avocados

juice of 1 lime

1 red chilli, finely chopped

50 g (1 cup) chopped coriander leaves

pinch of ground cumin

salt flakes and freshly ground black pepper

Tahini dressing

65 g (¼ cup) tahini

juice of 1 lemon

½ teaspoon paprika

salt flakes and freshly ground black pepper

Preheat the oven to 180°C.

Spread the sweet potato slices on a baking tray in a single layer, sprinkle with the cumin and cinnamon, then scatter over the pecans. Drizzle with the extra-virgin olive oil and maple syrup and season with salt and pepper, then bake for 40–50 minutes. The sweet spuds should be a bit crispy on the outside when they're ready.

While the potatoes are roasting, make your avo mash. Halve and stone the avocados and scoop the flesh into a large bowl. Add the remaining ingredients and mix well.

Remove the potatoes from the oven and let them cool a little while you make the dressing. Mix all the dressing ingredients together with 2–3 tablespoons of warm water in a little bowl.

Transfer the sweet spuds and pecans to a platter and serve with the dressing and mashed avo on the side. Top it all off with an extra drizzle of extra-virgin olive oil and a sprinkling of paprika – I get all fancy and sprinkle it from a height!

Serves 4

Up-beet brownie

There's something special about mixing beetroot and chocolate – it just works!
This recipe is a walk in the park and is a great way to sneak some liver-stimulating
beetroot into your diet, along with all those lovely antioxidants that give the beetroot
its awesome purple–red colour.

100 g (1 cup) almond meal
(I like the one made from
almonds with the skin on)

30 g (¼ cup) raw cacao
powder

140 g (1 cup) grated raw
beetroot, skin left on

3 large eggs

125 ml (½ cup) coconut oil,
melted

60 ml (¼ cup) maple syrup

1 teaspoon gluten-free
baking powder

1 vanilla pod, split and scraped
(or a pinch of vanilla powder
or a dash of vanilla extract)

Preheat the oven to 180°C and line a 28 cm x 18 cm
baking tray with baking paper.

Combine the almond meal and cacao powder in a large
bowl, then add all the other ingredients and mix well to
form a batter.

Pour the batter into the prepared baking tray and cook
for 20–25 minutes, or until a skewer inserted in the middle
comes out clean. Remove from the oven and allow to cool
before cutting into pieces.

Makes 16

Light and
bright meals

Summer nights salad

This salad is a cinch to make. It's something I whip up every single Christmas, and year after year it's the first thing to be gobbled up. Avocados are a good source of fibre, potassium and vitamin C, and although they are high in fat, it's the good kind. I definitely notice the more good fat in my diet, the better my skin and hair health is.

160 g (1 cup) macadamia nuts, activated if possible (see page 35)

2 large avocados, cubed

2 large mangoes, sliced

½ red onion, finely sliced

150 g rocket, washed and dried

75 g (½ cup) crumbled goat's feta, plus extra to serve

Dressing

zest and juice of 1 lime

80 ml (⅓ cup) extra-virgin olive oil

1 tablespoon wholegrain mustard

2 tablespoons raw honey, melted

salt flakes and freshly ground black pepper

Lightly toast the macadamias in a small frying pan over low heat for 1–2 minutes, shaking the pan so they toast evenly (you won't need to add any oil as they will release their own).

Place the avocado, mango and macadamias in a large bowl and mix. Add the onion and stir through gently. Lastly, add the rocket – make sure it's dry so it can soak up all the amazing flavours – and goat's feta and give it a very light toss with your fingers.

To make the dressing, whisk together the lime juice, lime zest, olive oil, mustard and honey in a small jug or bowl. Season to taste.

Pour the dressing over the salad and toss lightly with your fingertips so it coats everything but doesn't bruise the rocket leaves. Then top with a bit more goat's cheese and serve. I reckon this will be a favourite.

Serves 4–6

TIP
Soak your chia seeds for
5–10 minutes beforehand
to maximise the essential
fatty acid health benefits.
They will get a little gluggy,
but that's OK – it's all the
omega-3 goodness.

Empower-me super salad

This salad is about as clean as it gets; it's full of superfoods, it's vegan but also ticks the paleo boxes and it's an easy one to add protein to if you want. I love it because it's beautiful and bright, but most of all because it reminds me of a trip I went on to LA with one of my best mates, Andrea. We'd spend our days exploring all the raw food places, and I noticed that the superfood salads there had a few things in common: they were vegan, raw and contained dulse flakes, chia seeds and often apple cider vinegar. So here's my take on an LA-style superfood salad.

2 handfuls of baby spinach

2 handfuls of rocket

½ punnet (125 g) cherry tomatoes, halved

4 celery stalks, sliced on the diagonal

1 avocado, sliced

seeds of 1 pomegranate

1 tablespoon pumpkin seeds

1 tablespoon chia seeds

1 teaspoon dulse flakes

salt flakes and freshly ground black pepper

Dressing

1 tablespoon macadamia oil

2 teaspoons apple cider vinegar

Combine all the ingredients in a large salad bowl and dress with the macadamia oil and apple cider vinegar. Serve immediately and enjoy.

Serves 2

Raw vegan zucchini pasta with basil pesto

I love making this recipe for someone who's never had zucchini pasta before – they're always blown away that it's just raw zucchini. It does look great if you have a spiraliser but I don't have one in Sydney, so I just popped out and bought a 'green papaya grater' from an Asian supermarket for about $6 and it does the trick! As well as tasting delish, the pine nuts and cashews in the pesto are a brilliant source of healthy fats and veggie protein.

3 zucchini, peeled

Pesto

115 g (¾ cup) pine nuts, toasted

40 g (¼ cup) cashew nuts, activated if possible
(see page 35)

30 g (1 loosely packed cup) basil leaves (save a couple of small leaves for serving)

2 garlic cloves

zest and juice of 1 lemon

60 ml (¼ cup) extra-virgin olive oil, plus extra if needed

salt flakes and freshly ground black pepper

First, whip up the pesto by putting everything into a food processor or blender and blitzing until you have the texture you like (you may need to add a little more oil to get your desired consistency). Season it to taste and set aside.

For the pasta, finely slice the zucchini, using either a mandoline, a veggie spiraliser or green papaya grater, then put it all into a big bowl.

Mix the pesto through the pasta then plate up. Scatter a few baby basil leaves over the top and serve.

Serves 2

Mum's simple tomato salad

Tomatoes are full of lycopene, a potent antioxidant that is brilliant for protecting the heart from cardiovascular disease (it also makes the tomato red). As a kid, I remember Mum eating tomatoes like apples – taking a bite, then adding a pinch of salt, then another bite. This recipe is inspired by one she taught me early on and is just so simple to make.

1 punnet (250 g) heirloom cherry tomatoes, halved

4 tomatoes, cut into discs

1 bunch of basil, leaves picked

100 g sheep's feta

balsamic vinegar, to serve

extra-virgin olive oil, to serve

salt flakes and freshly ground black pepper

Choose the bowl or plate you want to serve the salad in, then place a layer of mixed heirloom cherry tomato halves and sliced tomatoes on the bottom.

Scatter over a layer of basil leaves, then crumble over a couple of chunks of feta. Now add a tiny drizzle of balsamic and another drizzle of extra-virgin olive oil. Repeat the layers over and over until your ingredients are used up and your bowl is full. Season with salt and pepper and give it one last drizzle of balsamic and olive oil.

Top with a few last basil leaves to make it look pretty. It still tastes great the next day too.

Serves 4

TIP
If you can't get a
conga spud, desiree
has a yummy, creamy
flesh and a pretty
pink skin.

Luna moon omelette

This recipe is a great way to get loads of veggies in. It also tastes ace and I reckon you could make it for any meal of the day. Eggs are little powerhouses when it comes to health and are full of protein, B vitamins, vitamin D, iron and zinc. Opt for free-range and organic eggs and add them to your diet wherever you can.

2 teaspoons butter

½ red onion, finely chopped

1 garlic clove, finely sliced

1 potato, thinly sliced (I love to use purple conga)

90 g (1 cup) sliced mushrooms (I like Swiss)

6 eggs, whisked

50 g (1 cup) baby spinach

70 g (½ cup) cherry tomatoes, quartered

small handful of chopped flat-leaf parsley, plus extra leaves to serve

salt flakes and freshly ground black pepper

Melt half the butter in a frying pan or heavy-based saucepan over a medium heat. Add the onion, garlic and spud and cook until translucent (2–3 minutes). Add the mushrooms and cook for a further minute. Remove the mixture from the pan and set aside.

In the same pan, melt the remaining butter over a medium heat and add the whisked egg, tilting the pan so it covers the base. Cook for 1–2 minutes. Spoon the potato mixture evenly over one half of the egg base, then sprinkle over the spinach, cherry tomato and parsley. Season with salt and pepper to taste. Now fold over the other side of the egg base. Garnish with extra parsley (coriander works well too) and serve.

Serves 2

Vegan caesar salad

✳

I love this as a main, on its own or as a side to chicken. You won't need to use all the chickpea croutons here, but it's so easy to make them up in a big batch, and you can add them to pretty much any other salad – a great way to get your veggo energy.

1 bunch of kale, stalks removed and leaves cut into thin ribbons

1 cos lettuce, chopped

1 teaspoon LSA

Chickpea croutons

2 tablespoons extra-virgin olive oil

1 fresh chilli, chopped (chilli flakes work too)

1 garlic clove, finely diced

¼ teaspoon cayenne pepper

1 x 400 g can chickpeas (or 1 cup dried chickpeas, soaked, rinsed and cooked)

salt flakes and freshly ground black pepper

Nut cheese

40 g (¼ cup) macadamia nuts (see Tips)

40 g (¼ cup) cashew nuts (see Tips)

½ garlic clove

salt flakes and freshly ground black pepper

Caesar dressing

80 g (½ cup) cashew nuts (see Tips)

60 ml (¼ cup) extra-virgin olive oil

1 teaspoon dijon mustard

1 garlic clove

zest and juice of 1 lemon

salt flakes and freshly ground black pepper

Preheat the oven to 180°C and line a baking tray with baking paper.

For the chickpea croutons, drizzle the olive oil over the prepared tray, add the remaining ingredients and roll everything around so that the chickpeas are coated evenly. Roast for 10 minutes then move the chickpeas around and cook for a further 10 minutes. You want them to be golden and crispy.

In the meantime, make your nut cheese. Pop all the ingredients into a blender or food processor and whizz it to the consistency of a crumbled cheese.

For the dressing, simply whizz together all the ingredients in your blender until smooth, season to taste with salt and pepper and add a little water at the end if you need to thin it out a bit.

To serve, put the kale and cos in a bowl, pour over the dressing and toss together well. In goes your nut cheese – give that a good old mix too – then add half the chickpea croutons and mix again. Top with a lucky last few croutons and a sprinkle of LSA for added texture.

Serves 2

TIPS
Try to use activated nuts for the nut cheese and dressing (see page 35).
Save the kale stalks to throw into your stir-fries and soups.
For a non-vegan option, add three chopped boiled eggs and a few anchovies.

Soba noodle salad with ginger and almond butter dressing

When I was studying this was my go-to recipe. My boyfriend at the time even learned how to make it, so he could have it waiting for me after a big day at uni. I loved it to the point I'd make it at least three nights a week, and sometimes I'd add fresh chilli on top too, which gives it nice punch and colour! When buying your noodles, read the packet carefully because you want them to be made from 100 per cent buckwheat (some add wheat, which I know my tummy reacts to).

250 g soba noodles

1 red capsicum, diced

1 carrot, grated

½ broccoli head, chopped into small florets

2 large handfuls of baby spinach

40 g (¼ cup) roughly chopped almonds, activated if possible (see page 35)

¼ bunch of basil, leaves picked and chopped

¼ bunch of coriander, leaves picked and chopped

Dressing

125 g (½ cup) almond butter

60 ml (¼ cup) apple cider vinegar

1 tablespoon maple syrup

2 cm piece of ginger, grated

2 teaspoons tamari

salt flakes and freshly ground black pepper, to taste

1 garlic clove

zest and juice of 1 lemon

Pop the noodles into simmering water and cook them according to the packet instructions – it's usually about 6 minutes.

Strain the noodles, transfer them to a large bowl and immediately toss through your veggies. I love to let them cook slightly in the hot noodles.

To make the dressing, just add the ingredients to a blender or food processor and whizz everything together. If you want it thinned out a little more, try adding 2 tablespoons of water. Toss enough dressing through the salad to coat the noodles and veggies, then serve up in bowls and top with the chopped almonds, basil and coriander.

Serves 2

TIP
This is a big batch of dressing, so you should have some left over. It tastes great on pretty much any salad – I tossed it through a quinoa salad the other day and it worked a treat.

95

TIP
Sometimes I add a
protein like crispy
salmon, poached chicken
or even a couple of fried
eggs to this. I love it with
fried eggs!

Cauli and parsnip fried rice

The first time I tried this, I was blown away by the texture of the cauliflower and parsnip rice. It's pretty awesome and so much like the real thing, but stuffed full of all the nutritional benefits of these two great veggies, along with loads of extra fibre to help keep your digestive system happy! You can tweak the ingredients to make the flavours work for you.

1 cauliflower, chopped into small chunks

2 parsnips, roughly chopped

1 tablespoon extra-virgin olive oil, plus extra to serve

½ onion (brown or red), finely diced

1 garlic clove, finely chopped

4 celery stalks, chopped (leaves reserved to serve)

1 red capsicum, diced

1 zucchini, grated

1 carrot, grated

60 g (1 cup) chopped broccoli

salt flakes and freshly ground black pepper

1 tablespoon tamari

1 chilli, chopped

Pop the cauliflower chunks and chopped parsnip into a food processor and pulse together to a rice-like consistency.

Heat the olive oil in a deep frying pan or wok over a medium heat, add the onion and garlic and sauté for a minute or so, then add your cauli and parsnip rice and sauté for another 5 minutes.

Throw in the rest of the veggies, toss them through and cook for just a few minutes, then remove from the heat. Season to taste, drizzle over the tamari, scatter over the chopped chilli and reserved celery leaves and serve.

Serves 4

No-nonsense Niçoise

This is a pretty popular salad. I love it because it's quick, delicious and makes enough for lunch the next day. The tuna and eggs give you all the protein you need and all those amazing veg colours mean you're also taking on board a truckload of phytochemicals (that's just a fancy way of saying healthy plant nutrients). Yum!

large handful of green beans, topped and tailed

1 small cos lettuce, roughly chopped

12 black olives, pitted and chopped

4 tomatoes, quartered

4 eggs, hard-boiled, peeled, cooled and halved

½ red onion, thinly sliced

1 red capsicum, sliced

8 salted anchovies (optional)

1 x 285 g can tuna in oil or spring water, drained (I love the one in chilli oil, as it gives a nice flavour twang)

salt flakes and freshly ground black pepper

Dressing

½ teaspoon dijon mustard

1 tablespoon red wine vinegar

2½ tablespoons extra-virgin olive oil

Cook the beans in salted boiling water for around 2 minutes until tender yet crisp. (They'll brighten up a smidge when they're perfect and ready to go.) Drain, refresh in cold water, drain again and set aside.

To make the dressing, combine the mustard and red wine vinegar in a small bowl. Whisk while slowly adding the olive oil and continue whisking until creamy and emulsified.

Combine the remaining salad ingredients with the beans and a little salt and pepper in a large bowl. Drizzle over the dressing and give it a good toss. Divide among four plates and serve.

Serves 4

TIP
I use a green papaya grater
to get the long strips – they're
about $6 at an Asian grocer.
A potato peeler can do
the job but you'll end up
with ribbons rather
than thin strips.

Green papaya salad

This is my take on the classic South-East Asian green papaya salad. Green papaya is packed with nutrients like potassium, magnesium and vitamins A, B and C – making it not only super tasty, but super healthy too. I like this with a lovely piece of white fish, some prawns cooked in coconut oil or even some shredded chicken. But it's full of flavour all on it's own, too, so if you're vegan or veggo it should hit the mark.

1 green papaya, halved, peeled and cut into long, thin strips

2 carrots, grated

30 g (¼ cup) dried cranberries

70 g (½ cup) cherry tomatoes, halved

½ bunch of mint, leaves picked and finely chopped

80 g (½ cup) cashew nuts, activated if possible (see page 35), roughly chopped

Dressing

60 ml (¼ cup) apple cider vinegar

60 ml (¼ cup) tamari

2 teaspoons coconut sugar

To serve

1 teaspoon black or white sesame seeds

1 red chilli, chopped (optional)

¼ bunch of coriander, leaves picked and chopped

This one is so simple; just pop all the salad ingredients in a bowl and give them a good old mix, then make your dressing in a little bowl or jar.

Pour half the dressing over your salad and dress well (leave the remaining half in the fridge for the next time you make this salad – it should last for about a week). Then sprinkle with sesame seeds, chilli (if using) and coriander and share it with a mate.

Serves 2 as a main or 4 as a side

Dressings

✳

Dressings are a brilliant way to up the flavour and add a few health benefits to your creations through the use of spices. You can make them in advance and store them in the fridge until needed (where you can also keep leftovers if you have any).

Sheep's yoghurt dressing

125 g (½ cup) plain sheep's yoghurt

2 tablespoons lemon juice

2 tablespoons wholegrain mustard

30 g (½ cup) dill fronds, roughly chopped

salt flakes and freshly ground black pepper

Combine the yoghurt, lemon juice, mustard and dill in a small bowl or jug and season with salt and pepper to taste.

Balsamic dressing

170 ml (⅔ cup) extra-virgin olive oil

80 ml (⅓ cup) balsamic vinegar

pinch of freshly ground black pepper

1 garlic clove, crushed

4 basil leaves, finely chopped

Combine all the ingredients in a small bowl or jug. Mix well as the balsamic and oil will naturally separate.

Simple wholegrain mustard dressing

125 ml (½ cup) extra-virgin olive oil

60 ml (¼ cup) lemon juice

1 heaped tablespoon wholegrain mustard

pinch each of salt flakes and freshly ground black pepper

Combine all the ingredients in a small bowl or jug.

Avocado cream dressing

1 large avocado (I use Hass)

1 tablespoon tahini

60 ml (¼ cup) lemon juice

60 ml (¼ cup) extra-virgin olive oil

pinch of paprika

pinch each of salt flakes and freshly ground black pepper

Pop all the ingredients into a blender (a food processor will do the trick too) then pour into a bowl, and you're ready to serve.

Lemon dressing

zest and juice of 1 lemon

60 ml (¼ cup) extra-virgin olive oil

pinch each of salt flakes and freshly ground black pepper

Simply combine all the ingredients together. This one will last a full week in the fridge.

Pomegranate dressing

2 tablespoons pure pomegranate juice

2 tablespoons pomegranate seeds

60 ml (¼ cup) extra-virgin olive oil

salt flakes and freshly ground black pepper, to taste

Mix all the ingredients together, then you're good to go.

Hardcore prawn salad

✳

There are two people who have inspired this salad. One is my mate Jad, who used to make this for me when we worked at Prahran Health Foods together (we'd often spend our days coming up with new food inventions and this one was so, so, so good). And the other is Lara, a Melbourne-based fashion designer, who has a top with a picture of a prawn on it with the words 'Hardcore Prawn', which I thought was pretty cheeky. I love using prawns as a source of protein – they're full of flavour!

3 small red chillies

1 tablespoon coconut oil

½ onion, sliced

1 kg raw prawns, peeled and deveined

1 heaped tablespoon gluten-free
tom yum paste

1 tablespoon gluten-free tamarind paste

freshly ground black pepper

2 carrots, peeled into ribbons

4 celery stalks, finely sliced

1 bunch of coriander
(including stalks), chopped

1 large bunch of Vietnamese mint, leaves
picked and sliced into thin ribbons

2 small yellow summer squash, grated

zest and juice of 2 large limes

3–4 tablespoons fish sauce

5–8 drops of stevia or 2 teaspoons
coconut syrup

2–3 teaspoons sesame oil

200 g bean thread vermicelli
or kelp noodles

2 teaspoons macadamia oil (optional)

handful of crushed cashew nuts,
activated if possible (see page 35)

Finely dice two of the small red chillies (reserve the last one for the salad). Heat the coconut oil in a heavy-based frying pan over a medium heat. Add the onion, diced chilli and prawns. Stir in the tom yum paste, tamarind paste and a couple of twists of pepper and cook for 5 minutes, stirring with a wooden spoon. When the prawns are cooked through, remove the pan from the heat and leave to cool.

Combine the carrot, celery, coriander, mint and squash in a large bowl and set aside.

Combine the lime zest and juice, fish sauce, stevia (or coconut syrup), sesame oil and remaining diced chilli in a small bowl and whisk with a fork. Adjust the flavours to taste.

Prepare the noodles according to the packet instructions and toss through the veggies and the dressing. Add the macadamia oil if desired (sometimes the sesame is all you need).

When the prawns are cool or warm (not hot), toss them through the dressed noodle salad and top with the crushed cashews.

Serves 6

Barbecued salmon with Aussie, Aussie salad

This is bright, healthy and, most importantly, tasty. Salmon is a great way to up the omega-3s in your diet. But the good fats are found in the skin, so keep it on – when it's crispy it tastes unbelievable. And you've gotta love a green and gold salad.

4 x 200 g salmon fillets
(skin on)

salt flakes and freshly ground
black pepper

2 tablespoons coconut oil,
melted

zest and juice of 1 lime

1 mango, cubed

1 avocado, sliced

75 g (½ cup) crumbled
goat's feta

2 tablespoons pumpkin seeds

100 g (2 cups) baby spinach

½ chilli, thinly sliced on the
diagonal (you can leave this
out if you're not a fan of heat
– I'm hooked on it)

2 tablespoons extra-virgin
olive oil

Preheat a chargrill or barbecue to medium–high. Season the salmon with salt and pepper, drizzle with a little coconut oil and sprinkle over the lime zest. Cook, skin-side up, for 3 minutes.

Turn and continue cooking for 4–6 minutes (depending on thickness), or until the salmon is just cooked through and the skin is crispy. Set the fillets aside to rest.

To make the salad, place the remaining ingredients in a bowl and lightly toss together. Serve alongside the salmon.

Serves 4

Summery san choy bow

This looks pretty special, and when I lived on the Gold Coast we used to make it all the time. It's bright, fresh and a great dish for when you're having mates over for a summer drink or two.

8 large iceberg lettuce leaves (these are your cups)

1 tablespoon sesame oil

250 g free-range chicken mince

1 tablespoon grated ginger

2 garlic cloves, finely chopped

1 red chilli, finely chopped

1 carrot, finely diced

1 capsicum, finely diced

60 ml (¼ cup) tamari

1 tablespoon rice wine vinegar

1 tablespoon lime juice

2 teaspoons coconut sugar

45 g (½ cup) bean sprouts

2 spring onions, trimmed and finely chopped

1 small bunch of coriander, leaves picked and roughly chopped

1 tablespoon sesame seeds, toasted

Trim the lettuce leaves and place in a bowl of cold water to chill for 10 minutes, then drain and set aside.

While the lettuce is chilling, heat the sesame oil in a wok or large frying pan over a high heat. Add the chicken mince and sauté until just cooked through, breaking up any large clumps with a wooden spoon.

Stir in the ginger, garlic and chilli, then add the carrot and capsicum and cook for a further 4 minutes, stirring constantly, until the vegetables have softened slightly. Stir in the tamari, rice wine vinegar, lime juice and coconut sugar.

Continue stirring until the sugar dissolves, then remove from the heat and add the sprouts, spring onion and coriander. Mix well.

To serve, spoon the mince and veggie mixture into the lettuce cups and sprinkle with sesame seeds.

Serves 4

TIP
This tastes equally delish
if you use turkey, beef
or lamb mince instead
of chicken. You can play
around with different herbs
and spices, too!

Sardinia salad

✳

Sardines are probably my favourite fish, and not just because they contain bucket-loads of super-healthy omega-3 fatty acids, which are brilliant both for the brain and for cardiovascular health. I love them fresh or tinned. This quinoa salad is pretty nutrient dense, and I like to use a combo of all three colours – red, white and black – for it, but it will work with just one if that's all you have on hand.

200 g (1 cup) quinoa, cooked and cooled

1 Lebanese cucumber, diced

1 punnet (250 g) cherry tomatoes, halved

2 spring onions, trimmed and finely chopped

1 carrot, peeled and grated

1 raw beetroot, peeled and grated

25 g (¼ cup) flaked almonds, toasted, plus extra to serve

salt flakes and freshly ground black pepper

8 whole sardines, scaled and gutted

coconut oil, for brushing

handful of roughly chopped flat-leaf parsley leaves (optional)

lemon wedges, to serve

Dressing

60 ml (¼ cup) extra-virgin olive oil

zest and juice of 1 lemon

1 tablespoon maple syrup

1 garlic clove, crushed

Place the quinoa, cucumber, tomatoes, spring onion, carrot, beetroot and almonds in a large bowl and toss to combine.

To make the dressing, in a separate small bowl whisk together the olive oil, lemon zest and juice, maple syrup and garlic. Pour the dressing over the salad, season with salt and pepper and mix well. Set aside until ready to serve.

Wash the sardines and pat dry. Brush with coconut oil and season all over with salt and pepper. Heat a griddle pan, frying pan or barbecue grill and cook the sardines over a very high heat for 3–4 minutes, turning once halfway through. The sardines should be cooked through and slightly charred.

Divide the salad among four plates and top each with two sardines. Sprinkle with parsley (if using) and extra flaked almonds, and serve with lemon wedges. Job done, and I think this one looks pretty impressive, too.

Serves 4

Superfood crispy salmon stir-fry

✳

I love quick and easy meals that are going to nourish me but also taste awesome.
This one's great because you can make a big batch and have lunch for the next couple
of days sorted. It's stuffed with fantastic nutrients, and the salmon and chia seeds in
particular are full of omega-3 fatty acids, which makes them perfect brain food.
If salmon isn't your thing, you can replace it with prawns, beef, chicken … or pretty
much any protein source that takes your fancy.

2 tablespoons coconut oil

1 garlic clove, diced

½ red onion, sliced

2 x 150 g salmon fillets (skin
on), cut into bite-sized chunks

2 handfuls of kale, stalks
removed and leaves roughly
chopped

60 g (1 cup) broccoli florets

handful of slivered almonds,
to serve (if you can't find
slivered, roughly chopped
is totally fine)

1 teaspoon chia seeds

Melt the coconut oil in a frying pan over a medium heat.
Pop the garlic and onion in the pan and wait for them to
soften, then in goes your salmon. Stir-fry for 3–4 minutes
until the skin goes crispy, then in goes your kale (you don't
want the kale to be too wet, so I like to give it a quick
towel dry before it goes in). Cook for another couple of
minutes until the kale goes crispy too.

Add the broccoli and cook for just another minute or so,
until the broccoli goes super bright. Then dish up into
bowls and top with the almonds and chia seeds. Enjoy!

Serves 2

Kangaroo fillets with sautéed kale

✳

Kangaroo is a particularly healthy type of red meat, with plenty of iron and vitamin B12 but virtually no fat. It does have a much stronger flavour than that of beef steaks, so know that you can use any meat in the place of kanga in this recipe. And this kale creation is such a yummy side, you can serve it with almost anything.

4 x 150–200 g kangaroo fillets

2 tablespoons extra-virgin olive oil, butter or coconut oil

salt flakes and freshly ground black pepper

200 g (3 cups) kale leaves, stalks removed

2 garlic cloves, finely chopped

3 anchovy fillets, drained

1 small red chilli, chopped

2 tablespoons pine nuts, lightly toasted

Preheat the oven to 220°C. Rub the kangaroo fillets with 1 tablespoon of oil or butter and season with a pinch of salt and pepper.

Heat a heavy-based frying pan over a medium–high heat and seal the kangaroo fillets for 1 minute on each side, then transfer to a baking tray and cook for 4 minutes in the oven. Remove from the oven and place on a warmed plate. Cover with foil and leave to rest.

Place the kale in a pot of lightly salted, boiling water and cook for 3 minutes. Drain well and set aside.

Using the same frying pan, sauté the garlic with the remaining oil or butter. Add the anchovy fillets and chilli and stir for a couple of minutes until the anchovies have dissolved. Add the drained kale leaves and pine nuts and sauté for 5 minutes.

Slice and serve the rested kangaroo fillets with the sautéed kale. Enjoy.

Serves 4

Beef n' broc stir-fry

✳

This may not be the prettiest dish but it tastes great and it's brilliant for you. I cook
with broccoli nearly every day – it helps out the liver, which acts as the garbage man
for the entire body by removing toxins and cleaning the blood. I love eating food that
gives you a mini liver detox without you even knowing! I grew up thinking broccoli
heads were fairies' homes thanks to my babysitter Linda, who would always get me to
eat them by telling me about the magical fairy power I would gain if I did.

60 ml (¼ cup) extra-virgin
olive oil

400 g beef mince (organic
and/or grass-fed is best)

1 red onion, sliced

155 g (1 cup) cashew nuts,
activated if possible
(see page 35), toasted

3 cm piece of ginger, grated

1 garlic clove, grated

salt flakes and freshly ground
black pepper

¼ cauliflower head, chopped
into florets

1 red capsicum, sliced

½ broccoli head, chopped
into florets

40 g (¼ cup) black sesame
seeds, toasted (if you can't
find the black ones, white will
do just fine)

Heat a frying pan or wok over a medium heat, add the
olive oil then the beef and stir-fry until it's browned.
Add the onion, cashews, ginger and garlic and toss about
for a couple of minutes until the onion and garlic soften.
Season with salt and pepper, then add the cauliflower and
give it another stir about. Finally, in goes the capsicum and
broccoli right at the end because I love them to be really
nice and crunchy!

Sprinkle with the toasted sesame seeds and enjoy. Any
leftovers are great for lunch, too.

Serves 4

Summery
sweet treats

Mint, cucumber and mango granita

This is the perfect summery treat – tropical and so fresh with the mint and cucumber. The mint aids digestion, so it's a great one to have after a summer night's barbecue.

2 mangoes, diced
(fresh is best but frozen
still does the trick)

1 cucumber, skin on,
roughly chopped

½ bunch of mint, leaves
picked and chopped

250 ml (1 cup) coconut water

zest and juice of 1 lime

2 tablespoons coconut sugar
(or 4 drops of stevia, or a
pinch of stevia powder)

Pop everything into a food processor, blender or thermomix and whizz together until it forms a puree. Tip the mixture into a large baking dish and place it in the freezer for 2–3 hours, scraping it each hour with a fork until it's super chunky and granita-like. Portion into pretty glasses or bowls, and serve.

Serves 2

TIP
I also love this
on top of paleo
pancakes.

Fig, walnut and ginger ice cream

This feels like the most indulgent dessert, but it's a walk in the park to make and it's so healthy! The figs are full of nutrients and antioxidants, while the ginger is great for digestion – just what you need at the end of a meal. I've been known to whip this up for brekkie too … it's just too yummy! You'll need to start start this recipe the day before.

6 fresh figs, quartered, then frozen overnight

200 ml coconut milk

1 tablespoon maple syrup

30 g (¼ cup) chopped walnuts, activated if possible (see page 35)

2 cm piece of ginger

pinch of ground cinnamon

Toppings

4 fresh figs, sliced into discs or ripped up (depending on whether you want insta-pretty or rustic)

grated dark chocolate (raw or at least 70% cacao solids)

Put everything except the topping ingredients in a food processor, blender or thermomix and blend together well.

The ice cream will be ready to eat straight away, or you can pop it in the freezer for another hour and then enjoy. Top with extra fresh figs and grated chocolate to make it look really impressive – the perfect date dessert!

Serves 2

Salted caramel, chocolate and date frozen fudge

The title says it all – this is the perfect combo of chocolate and salted caramel, which always hits the spot. It's also packed with dates, which are full of potassium for heart health and fibre for healthy digestion. The only problem with this recipe, if you're anything like me, is that it's so hard not to go back for seconds. Or thirds. Or even fourths!

1 frozen banana (peel it before you freeze it)

1 teaspoon raw cacao powder

2 medjool dates, pitted

1 tablespoon almond butter

pinch of salt flakes

60 ml (¼ cup) almond milk, plus extra if needed

Toppings

chopped pitted medjool dates

dried white mulberries

chopped walnuts, activated if possible (see page 35)

raw cacao powder

Pop everything into a blender and whizz together until smooth – if you need more almond milk to get your desired consistency, then add another 60 ml (¼ cup) or so and keep blending until you're happy. Divide between two glasses or cute little serving jars, then place them in your freezer for 10 minutes to let it really thicken up.

Top with any or all of the topping ingredients and serve.

Serves 2

TIP
There's no need to store
these in the fridge – I store
them in an airtight container
in my pantry. I get 2–3 days
out of them, but that's only if
they don't get gobbled up
straight away.

Monster chocolate cupcakes with spirulina icing

My friend Karina (who styles all the books I write and is one very talented soul) helped me with this one, and they are probably some of the best-tasting cupcakes I've had. You wouldn't know they're paleo at all – it doesn't feel like you're missing out on a thing!

60 g (½ cup) coconut flour

60 g (½ cup) raw cacao powder

½ teaspoon salt

½ teaspoon bicarbonate of soda

200 g (1 cup) coconut sugar

6 eggs

125 ml (½ cup) coconut oil, melted

edible flowers, to serve (optional)

Spirulina icing

600 g (3 cups) coconut sugar

100 g butter, softened

60 ml (¼ cup) almond milk

1 teaspoon spirulina powder (barley greens or chlorella would also do the trick; it's for colour, not flavour)

Preheat the oven to 180°C. Line nine holes of a regular muffin tin with patty cases.

In a medium-sized bowl, combine the coconut flour, cacao, salt, bicarbonate of soda and coconut sugar. In a separate large bowl, whisk together the eggs and melted coconut oil. Add the egg mixture to the dry ingredients and mix until well combined.

Pour the mixture evenly into the cupcake liners and bake for 15–18 minutes, or until a skewer inserted into the middle comes out clean. Cool for 5 minutes in the tin, then remove and place on wire racks to cool completely.

For the icing, place the coconut sugar – in batches – in a mini food processor or spice grinder and whizz to a fine powder. Using an electric mixer, cream the butter in a large bowl until it is soft and pale. Gradually add the powdered coconut sugar while beating. Add the almond milk and spirulina and continue beating until well combined.

Spread the icing onto the cooled cupcakes and decorate with edible flowers, if you fancy.

Makes 9

Mango and coconut paleo loaf

※

To me, there's something really magical about the combination of mango and coconut. From a nutritional perspective, this loaf ticks all the paleo boxes, too. I've used teff flour in this recipe, which is a gluten-free Ethiopian grain that looks a bit like baby quinoa in its raw state and packs a serious iron punch (if you can't find it, quinoa flour works great in its place). I like to slice and freeze this loaf (after I've had a piece warm from the oven!), then when I'm ready I'll toast it and enjoy with macadamia butter, a dash of maple syrup and a sprinkle of cinnamon.

185 ml (¾ cup) coconut oil, melted

200 g (2 cups) almond meal

60 g (½ cup) coconut flour

80 g (½ cup) teff flour

2 teaspoons gluten-free baking powder (any health-food store will stock this)

4 eggs

60 ml (¼ cup) almond milk

1 teaspoon ground cinnamon

1 vanilla pod, split and scraped (or ¼ teaspoon of the powdered jazz)

60 ml (¼ cup) maple syrup (or raw honey, coconut nectar or rice malt syrup)

2 super-ripe bananas, roughly mashed

60 g (1 cup) shredded coconut, plus extra to decorate

370 g (2 cups) cubed mango (fresh or frozen)

Preheat the oven to 180°C. Grease a 20 cm loaf tin with a third of the coconut oil (about 60 ml).

Mix the almond meal, flours and baking powder together in a big bowl. Add the rest of the coconut oil and the eggs, almond milk, cinnamon, vanilla and maple syrup and mix until well combined. Stir in the mashed banana, then gently fold through the shredded coconut and mango cubes.

Spoon the mixture into your loaf tin and sprinkle with a few more shards of coconut. Bake for 30–40 minutes – it should be golden on top, and you can always poke it in the middle with a skewer to check it's perfectly cooked (the skewer should come out clean). Let it cool a little in the tin and then enjoy while still warm. The house should smell pretty good!

Makes 1 delishimo loaf

'Cherry ripe' muffins

✳

As much as I'd love to claim this recipe as my own, it was something I was lucky enough to taste while visiting Gaia Retreat and Spa near Byron Bay last year. It blew me away that a healthy treat could taste so good. At Gaia they're all about sourcing locally and often growing their own food, so I was like a kid in a candy store, loving every single second of it! The head chef Dan Trewartha shared this recipe with me — it's a great Christmassy treat when cherries are in full swing.

70 g (⅔ cup) almond meal

60 g (⅔ cup) desiccated coconut

85 g (⅔ cup) gluten-free self-raising flour

1 teaspoon baking powder

1 teaspoon xanthan gum

150 g (1 cup) roughly chopped good-quality dark chocolate (at least 70% cacao solids)

pinch of salt flakes

125 ml (½ cup) coconut oil

1 banana, mashed

170 ml (⅔ cup) coconut milk or cream

80 ml (⅓ cup) freshly squeezed orange juice

3 eggs, beaten

1 tablespoon vanilla extract

200 g (1 cup) pitted cherries, halved

30 g (½ cup) shredded coconut

Preheat the oven to 200°C. Grease a regular 12-hole muffin tin with a little coconut oil and line with patty cases.

Place the almond meal, desiccated coconut, self-raising flour, baking powder, xanthan gum, chocolate and salt in a bowl and whisk to combine.

Place the coconut oil, banana, coconut milk or cream, orange juice, eggs and vanilla in a separate bowl and whisk to combine. Stir through the cherries, then fold the mixture through the combined dry ingredients to form a batter.

Spoon the batter evenly into the patty cases and top with a good sprinkle of shredded coconut. Reduce the oven temperature to 180°C and bake for 20 minutes, turning the tray around halfway through. Check one of the muffins with a skewer — if it comes out clean, they're ready; if not, cook for another 3 minutes, then test again.

When ready, remove the muffins from the oven and leave to cool on a wire rack before serving.

Makes 12

TIP
If cherries aren't in
season, this recipe also
works really well with
fresh strawberries,
raspberries or any
other berry.

TIP
Feel free to replace any
of the berries with ones
you prefer (or can find).
Frozen berries work
just as well. This is also
delicious with yoghurt.

Blissed out berry and apple crumble

✳

This berry and apple crumble is pretty awesome. The blueberries and raspberries are loaded with antioxidants and vitamin C, the apples are full of fibre and pectin, while the maca nuts and hazelnut meal are great sources of good fats. Yumbo!

310 g (2 cups) blueberries

125 g (1 cup) raspberries

4 granny smith apples, diced (I keep the peel on 'cos I like it chewy)

1 vanilla pod, split and scraped

zest and juice of 1 lime

50 g (¼ cup) coconut sugar (double the quantity if you prefer it sweeter)

50 g (½ cup) rolled oats (replace with quinoa flakes if you can't tolerate oats)

30 g (¼ cup) hazelnut meal (or almond meal)

15 g (¼ cup) shredded coconut

80 g (½ cup) roughly chopped macadamia nuts, activated if possible (see page 35)

125 ml (½ cup) coconut oil, melted

coconut ice cream, to serve (optional)

Preheat the oven to 180°C.

Combine the berries, apple, vanilla seeds, lime juice and zest and half the coconut sugar in a large bowl. Mix well with your hands (get those mitts in there!).

In another bowl, combine the oats, hazelnut meal, shredded coconut and macadamias.

Give them a stir, then add the coconut oil and the rest of the coconut sugar. Mix with your hands until the mixture is nice and crumbly.

Spoon the berry mixture into a baking dish (or divide among six individual ramekins). Spread the crumble mixture over the fruit and bake for 20–30 minutes, or until the top is golden and the berries are oozing a little.

Serve with a scoop of coconut ice cream and a sprinkling of freshly torn mint leaves, if you like.

Serves 6

Magic matcha and lime raw cake

This raw cake is high in antioxidants and is super refreshing. I figure, we're running about like crazy and are often pretty stressed out, so why not take all the antioxidant help we can get to help boost our immune systems and keep that stress at bay? This one works so well as mini cakes, too.

Base

160 g (1 cup) macadamia nuts, activated if possible (see page 35)

155 g (1 cup) cashew nuts, activated if possible (see page 35)

2 tablespoons raw cacao powder

8 medjool dates, pitted

2 tablespoons cashew butter (or macadamia or almond butter)

pinch of salt flakes

Filling

465 g (3 cups) cashew nuts, activated if possible (see page 35)

125 ml (½ cup) lime juice

170 ml (⅔ cup) coconut oil, melted

170 ml (⅔ cup) maple syrup

1 teaspoon matcha green tea powder, plus extra if needed

zest of 1 lime

To serve

1 lime, cut into super-thin slices

edible flowers (optional)

You'll need a 20 cm springform cake tin for this one.

Put the base ingredients in a food processor and blitz until the mixture is sticky (you may need to add up to 2 tablespoons of water to help it bind), then press it into the base of the cake tin. Pop the base in the freezer while you make the filling.

For the filling, blend the ingredients in a food processor or blender until really smooth. How long it takes will depend on how powerful your food processor or blender is – you just need to give it a little love, care and time. Be patient – it can take 3–5 minutes. Now have a taste and add more matcha tea if you want it stronger in flavour. Pour the creamy green tea and lime filling onto the base, then freeze for 4 hours.

When you're ready to serve, pop the super-thin slices of lime on top and decorate with edible flowers, if you like. Let the cake come to room temperature and tuck in!

Serves 12

Drinks
to uplift
and refresh

Green tea elixir

Matcha green tea powder is a popular superfood at the moment and it's full of so many goodies – number one being antioxidants – that I love including it in my diet. Adding the cinnamon was the idea of my recipe tester Bec, who thought it made this extra delish.

500 ml (2 cups) almond milk (coconut milk works well too)

½ teaspoon matcha green tea powder

stevia, to taste

ground cinnamon, to serve

Gently heat the almond milk and matcha powder in a small saucepan over a low heat. Add a drop or two of stevia to taste – it's powerful stuff so take it slow.

Once hot, divide the green tea elixir between two cups or mugs, dust with a sprinkling of cinnamon and serve.

Serves 2

Cheeky monkey

I love a great banana smoothie and this one is my go-to. Sometimes I add carob or cacao powder to it if I'm keen to bring in another element of flavour, and if I'm having it for brekkie and I know I have a huge day ahead, I'll add a handful of oats. It's my all-time favourite banana smoothie.

2 frozen bananas (peel them before you freeze them)

handful of macadamia nuts, activated if possible (see page 35), plus extra to serve

½ teaspoon ground cinnamon, plus extra to serve

¼ teaspoon ground nutmeg

1 teaspoon raw honey (or maple syrup or a few drops of stevia)

500 ml (2 cups) almond milk (any nut milk or drinking coconut milk also works well)

Pop everything into your blender and whizz together. Pour into two large or three small glasses and top with a sprinkle of cinnamon and a few extra chopped macas. Perfect!

Serves 2–3

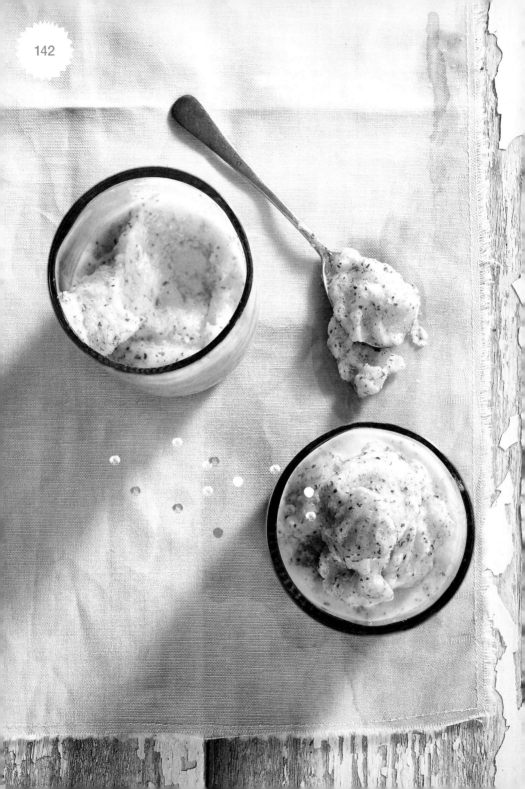

Minty-pine goodness

This drink pretty much sums up summer, but it's more than just zesty and refreshing. The pineapple is packed full of bromelain, which is both a great anti-inflammatory and a protein-digesting enzyme, making this brilliant after a heavy meal to help with digestion. Plus, the coconut water is loaded with electrolytes – I call it Mother Nature's sports drink. If you're having a few mates over, it's also a great one to add alcohol to (vodka works really well) and those electrolytes should even help prevent a hangover!

320 g (2 cups) roughly chopped pineapple, frozen

250 ml (1 cup) coconut water

¼ bunch of mint, leaves picked

zest and juice of 1 lime

2 medjool dates, pitted (or sweeten with maple syrup, raw honey, or a few drops of stevia or monk fruit extract)

70 g (½ cup) ice cubes

Pop all the ingredients in the blender and process until it looks like a slurpee (you don't want this one silky smooth).

Pour into two glasses or bowls and enjoy.

Serves 2

TIP
Pop any leftover
mixture into ice block
moulds, freeze it and
enjoy it later as
a cooling treat.

Sunset slushie

This recipe is an excellent source of vitamin C, lycopene and bioflavonoids, which means your skin will love it. In summer, we're naturally going to be exposed to more sunshine, so this is a great one to be drinking then, when your skin will really benefit from that extra protection and support.

300 g (2 cups) roughly chopped watermelon (keep the white rind on, as it's full of bioflavonoids), frozen

1 punnet (250 g) strawberries, frozen

handful of mint leaves

135–270 g (1–2 cups) ice cubes

Put all the ingredients in a blender and process until smooth. Divide between two glasses and enjoy.

Serves 2

Strawberry, basil and kombucha fizz

Kombucha is a fermented tea full of probiotics that's great for your gut health. This is really important, as a happy gut is vital for your overall health. Often called 'the second nervous system', the gut helps to keep your immune system strong, and getting probiotics into your diet is a great way to keep your entire digestive system thriving. It's fine to use store-bought kombucha for this recipe, but if you're game, try making your own! There's a recipe in my last book, *The Happy Life*, or have a look online. This drink looks pretty festive, making it a great one for Chrissie brunches.

¼ punnet (60 g) strawberries, sliced into discs

6 basil leaves, torn

500 ml (2 cups) kombucha (store-bought or homemade)

Divide the strawberries and basil between two tall glasses and muddle them together in the bottom of the glasses with the end of a wooden spoon. Top up with the kombucha and serve.

Serves 2

TIP
You can make the tea
and fruit combo ahead
of time and store it in an
airtight jar in the fridge.
Then just mix with some
soda water whenever
you feel like a tasty
summer drink.

TIP
The Rosemary and
Lemon Spritzer is best
enjoyed with a straw,
so you don't end up
with a mouthful
of rosemary.

Summer spritzers

✳

Spritzers are a great way to spice up your drinks and add flavour in a quirky way, and when you make them super healthy like this, the nutritional benefits are in there too. Plus, you can make them look really pretty with berries, herbs and edible flowers.

Pomegranate and lime spritzer

250 ml (1 cup) pure pomegranate juice

250 ml (1 cup) hibiscus tea, cooled
(or soda water works well too)

zest and juice of 1 lime, plus extra lime
slices to serve

seeds of ½ pomegranate (or 1 punnet
of pomegranate seeds)

70 g (½ cup) ice cubes

Pop all the ingredients into a jug and stir to mix everything together. Pour into glasses and serve nice and cold with a few lime slices to garnish.

Serves 2

Lemon myrtle and plum spritzer

4 plums, finely sliced into slivers

½ punnet (60 g) blueberries

500 ml (2 cups) lemon myrtle tea, cooled

250 ml (1 cup) soda water

edible flowers, to serve (optional)

Add the plum slivers and blueberries to the cooled tea in a small jug and leave to sit for 5 minutes to infuse. Divide the mixture between two tall glasses and top up with soda water. Garnish with a few edible flowers (if using) and serve.

Serves 2

Rosemary and lemon spritzer

zest of 1 lemon plus juice of 2 lemons

1 teaspoon coconut sugar (or stevia –
I use 3 drops or a pinch of the powder)

2 rosemary sprigs (1 crushed, 1 snipped
in half for prettiness at the end)

70 g (½ cup) ice cubes

500 ml (2 cups) soda water

Combine the lemon juice and zest, coconut sugar and crushed rosemary sprig in a small jug and leave for 20 minutes for the flavours to infuse.

Fill two tall glasses with ice, then pour over the lemon juice mixture and top up with soda water. Garnish each with half a sprig of rosemary (I like to use it as a bit of a swizzler to mix everything up), then sip away!

Serves 2

Thanks

- Mary Small, for taking the chance on me. It really means so much, and it's you who makes this dream come to life.
- Clare Marshall, it's been a dream to work with you on this. I love every single second working together.
- Charlotte Ree, for being the world's best book publicist and an inspiration to work with!
- Armelle Habib, you're a massive part of the magic in this book, and I feel super blessed to be working with you again. It's like you can read my mind. So much fun working with you!
- Karina Duncan, I love watching you in action. You're truly amazing and put your heart into everything you do. It means the world.
- Michelle Mackintosh, working with you always brings such joy. You're like this magical fairy who comes onto set and sees things differently, and I know I speak for everyone when I say we love it. You light up a room.
- Simon Davis, thank you for making my words make sense and always making me laugh. You're a champion.
- Emma Roocke, you're one of the smiliest people I know, and I am so happy when I see you on set. You're a massive part of the dream team.
- Caroline Griffiths, thanks for your ace cooking on set. It was a joy to work with you.
- Kylie McAllester, thank you so much for cooking up a storm for us.
- Fotini Hatzis, you really blow me away with your hair and makeup talents, but even more so with how much of an amazing human you are.
- Steph Rooney, loved working with you. Thank you for helping me get all the fashion shots.
- Rochelle Seator, thanks for being so ace to shoot with. Such dedication to be shooting in that cold water, too! Love working together, let's do it again soon.
- Helena Holmgren, thank you for being such a huge help and for guarding all the clothes!
- Tim O'Keefe, always love working with you. You're super humble and way more talented than you know. It's an honour to work with you.
- Linda Raymond, my rock, love you to the moon and back.
- Dad, thank you for always believing in me no matter what. You're always in my corner, Daddio, and it means more to me that you'll ever know.
- Mum, for always being such a huge support.
- Tristan Smith, baby bro, for being my number-one supporter. I think you buy more books than anyone and it means loads.
- Oscar Gordon, where would I be without you? You are one of my all-time favourite souls and have a massive heart. I feel very lucky to have you in my life.

- Sophie Monk, you're a game changer and you light up a room. You've taught me that having a real heart is magic.
- Andrea Evans, thank you for sharing these adventures with me. You always inspire me to be my best, so thank you.
- Salvatore Malatesta, thank you for being a massive inspiration and mentor.
- Lach Ward, love working and going crystal shopping with you. You're a really good egg.
- Lauren Miller, through thick and thin you're always fighting for me. It means loads, thank you.
- Leonie Sutherland (Lee Lee), thank you for being a massive part of this journey. Here's to living our dreams.
- Marlene Richardson, Marls, it's been great working with you. Thanks for all your help.
- Nick Manuell, thank you for helping me loads and teaching me so much. I'm really grateful.
- Rivis Donnelly, you always welcome me with such warmth into Dymocks on Collins Street in Melbourne. You are one of the nicest people I've ever met.
- Hayley Van Spanje, I love working with you. More adventures, please!
- Jenni Ballard, thank you for always being such a huge help with everything. It means loads.
- Mel Tjoeng, I love capturing magic with you. Thank you so much for always making time for some kind of whimsical adventure with me. You're a very special human, Mellie.
- Charlie Goldsmith, CG, thanks for being a real mate. Always your number one spud.
- Maddie Dixon, you live from your heart and that's rare. Always live from that space.
- Leisel Jones, thanks for always having my back, chicken, and inspiring me truckloads.
- Jad Patrick, thanks for being my quirky nature bud. Go live those dreams, Jaddles.
- Reece Carter, love our nature adventures. Thank you for being such a brill soul, Reecey.
- Lucy Roach, I always have to thank the first person to ever take a chance on me. I will never forget you putting me on TV for the first time. Always grateful.
- Rebecca Rich, you're the best recipe tester going around!
- Bonnie and Neil, Charlie and Fenton, Glenn Tebble and Kaz Morton, your creations are so wonderful and it's a dream to shoot with them.
- Tigerlily, for the amazing outfits featured throughout this book and on the cover. It's been a dream working with you.
- Ange Cleary, for helping source some lovely outfits for the shoot.
- Auguste the Label, Bombshell Bay Swimwear, Husk, Mahiya, Mandy Br, Sunday Somewhere, Tigmi Trading, Tully Lou and Warriorsdivine, thank you for the sweet clothing and accessories for the shoot.

Index

A Plum book
First published in 2016 by
Pan Macmillan Australia Pty Limited
Level 25, 1 Market Street,
Sydney, NSW 2000, Australia

Level 1, 15–19 Claremont Street,
South Yarra, Victoria 3141, Australia

Design by Michelle Mackintosh
Typeset by Pauline Haas
Edited by Simon Davis
Index by Frances Paterson
Photography by Armelle Habib
Prop and food styling by Karina Duncan
Additional wardrobe styling by Ange Cleary
  (The Fashionable Gypsy)
Food preparation by Caroline Griffiths,
  Kylie McAllester and Emma Roocke
Colour reproduction by Splitting Image
  Colour Studio
Printed and bound in China by 1010 Printing
  International Limited

A CIP catalogue record for this book is available
from the National Library of Australia.

Please note that versions of some of the
recipes in this book have appeared previously
in *The Happy Cookbook*, *Lola Berry's Little Book of
Smoothies & Juices* and *The Happy Life*.

We advise that the information contained in this
book does not negate personal responsibility
on the part of the reader for their own health
and safety. It is recommended that individually
tailored advice is sought from your healthcare
or medical professional. The publishers and their
respective employees, agents and authors are
not liable for injuries or damage occasioned to
any person as a result of reading or following the
information contained in this book.

The publisher would like to thank the following
for their generosity in providing props and
clothing for the book: Auguste the Label,
Bombshell Bay Swimwear, Bonnie and Neil,
Charlie and Fenton, Glenn Tebble Homewares,
Husk, Kaz Morton Ceramics, Mahiya, Mandy Br,
Sunday Somewhere, Tigerlily, Tigmi Trading,
Tully Lou and Warriorsdivine.

10 9 8 7 6 5 4 3